Praise for *Child*

"Fulcrum Publishing has done a welcome service for the Colorado history community by reissuing this scarce and long-out-of-print human drama, *Children of the Storm*. The book related the events of late March 1931, when a ramshackle wooden school bus carrying twenty pupils and the bus driver crashed during a killer blizzard in desolate far southeastern Colorado. In the late 1990s, historian Ariana Harner and Colorado journalist/historian Clark Secrest located a handful of survivors, who spoke publicly for the first time about their deathly ordeal—and the resultant exploitation that they did not seek."

> —Thomas J. "Dr. Colorado" Noel,
> Prof. Emeritus of History,
> University of Colorado at Denver

"I was unaware of my true family history until I read this book. It was the biggest family secret, and when I was growing up, I heard only vague references to it. This book gives the truest account of the events that happened on that day as well as after: a true and long forgotten ghost story."

> —Bessie Hall, granddaughter
> of survivor Laura Huffaker

"*Children of the Storm* is a moving story of the past and a timely reminder of how, especially now, we live at the mercy of natural forces. This tale of tragedy and survival, bravery and exploitation, beautifully told, will enrich your sense of the world and forever color the way you contemplate an approaching winter storm."

> —William Haywood Henderson,
> author of *Augusta Locke*

"*Children of the Storm* is an absorbing tale of survival and resilience. More than that, Ariana Harner and Clark Secrest expertly examine the aftermath of tragedy, with its unsung heroes and disingenuous opportunists. This compelling journey to a time both familiar and remote continues to resonate today."

> —Gillian Klucas, author of Sudler Award–winning
> *Leadville: The Struggle to Revive an American Town*

"In late March 1931, newspapers across the country carried the story of twenty children stranded for thirty-three hours in a school bus during a brutal snowstorm on Colorado's Eastern Plains. A blizzard hit just as school was starting...

It's the subject of *Children of the Storm* ... by Ariana Harner and Clark Secrest, [who] interviewed the seven living survivors. They've done an excellent job of separating truth from newspaper hype and demolishing the seventy-year-old myth of the boy hero. The resulting story of horror and exploitation is far more interesting than the legend."

—Sandra Dallas, *New York Times* bestselling author

"*Children of the Storm* conjures up a community and a cast of characters, mostly children, facing the great defining tragedy of their lives. Written with a clean, novelistic voice, the story takes us to the heart of our own vulnerabilities in the face of many great forces—an indifferent, sometimes hostile, nature, the self-interested pressures of larger, institutional powers. We become so absorbed in this world, we may not even realize how avidly we're turning the page."

—Andrea Dupree, Co-founder and Program Director,
Lighthouse Writers Workshop

"To this day, communities in southeastern Colorado are showing the rest of us how to learn and heal from a near unimaginable tragedy—in this case, a tragedy dating back to the Great Depression. This is essential High Plains history, told with an unflinching eye and an abundance of compassion."

—Steve Grinstead, co-editor of
Western Voices: 125 Years of Colorado Writing

CHILDREN
OF THE
STORM

CHILDREN
OF THE
STORM

The True Story of the
Pleasant Hill School Bus Tragedy

Ariana Harner & Clark Secrest

Fulcrum Publishing
Wheat Ridge, Colorado

ON THE COVER: Carl Miller's 1929 Chevrolet farm truck / school bus as it was discovered north of Holly, March 27, 1931. The vehicle's hood is raised; wet wiring had prevented Miller from restarting the engine when the bus stalled in the roadside ditch. A side window was inadvertently broken as pupils exercised in an attempt to survive. Tire chains were installed only on the right rear wheel. When finally located after "thirty-three hours of hell," five pupils had frozen to death and fifteen were in grave danger. Miller perished in trying to seek help.

OPPOSITE: Today the vast plains north of Holly are broken by this solitary monument marking the location where Miller's wooden bus bumped to a halt on March 26, 1931.

Library of Congress Cataloging-in-Publication Data
Names: Harner, Ariana, author. | Secrest, Clark, 1937- author.
Title: Children of the storm : the true story of the Pleasant Hill School bus tragedy / Ariana Harner and Clark Secrest.
Other titles: True story of the Pleasant Hill School bus tragedy
Description: Second edition. | Golden, Colorado : Fulcrum Publishing, 2024. | Includes bibliographical references and index. | Summary: "Imagine being one of twenty children, ages seven to fourteen, stranded in a makeshift school bus for thirty-three hours during the worst blizzard to hit Colorado in more than fifty years. The gripping narrative of Children of the Storm leads you through this haunting experience. The morning of March 26, 1931, began with sixty-degree weather and students excitedly running to board Carl Miller's bus for their routine ride to the Pleasant Hill School. By the time they arrived at the pair of forlorn one-room schoolhouses, it was dark, windy, and cold-obvious signs of a spring snowstorm. Soon after, following the teachers' orders to drive the children to a nearby home for safety, Miller lost his sense of direction in the ensuing whiteout and lodged the bus in a ditch. When rescuers found the survivors a day and a half later, the blizzard had taken its deadly toll. The media avidly pursued the story, and the children became national and international celebrities. Ariana Harner and Clark Secrest have written the first comprehensive account of the tragedy, culling details from interviews, newspaper clippings, and archival documents. This is a tale of media exploitation, false heroism, lifelong heartbreak, and hard-won survival"-- Provided by publisher.
Identifiers: LCCN 2023053532 (print) | LCCN 2023053533 (ebook) | ISBN 9781682754757 (paperback) | ISBN 9781682754764 (ebook)
Subjects: LCSH: Kiowa County (Colo.)--History--20th century. | School bus accidents--Colorado--Kiowa County--History--20th century. | Blizzards--Colorado--Kiowa County--History--20th century. | Children's accidents--Colorado--Kiowa County--History--20th century. | School children--Colorado--Kiowa County--Biography. | Kiowa County (Colo.)--Biography. | BISAC: SOCIAL SCIENCE / Sociology / Social Theory | PSYCHOLOGY / Interpersonal Relations
Classification: LCC F782.K4 H37 2024 (print) | LCC F782.K4 (ebook) | DDC 978.8/93033--dc23/eng/20231213
LC record available at https://lccn.loc.gov/2023053532
LC ebook record available at https://lccn.loc.gov/2023053533

Printed in the United States of America
0 9 8 7 6 5 4 3 2 1

Cover Design by Kateri Kramer

Fulcrum Publishing • 3970 Youngfield Street • Wheat Ridge, Colorado 80033
(800) 992-2908 • (303) 277-1623 • www.fulcrumbooks.com

To Bobbie Brown, Kenneth Johnson, Carl Miller,
Mary Louise Miller, Louise Stonebraker,
and Arlo Untiedt.

And to their friends and classmates
whose voices froze
during those thirty-three hours.
Here is your story.

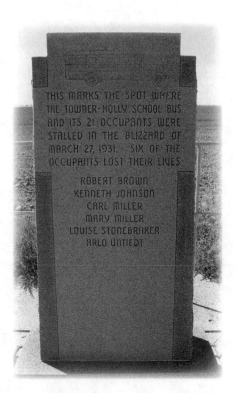

Contents

Foreword

ONE DAY: Thursday, March 26, 1931. Three places: the blizzard-swept plains of extreme southeastern Colorado, the palatial mansion of Frederick G. Bonfils in Denver, and the USS *Arizona* steaming north from Puerto Rico.

Onboard the *Arizona*, President Herbert Hoover enjoyed the day sailing through what *The New York Times* described as "slightly rolling turquoise seas in warm brilliant sunshine." After visits to the Virgin Islands and Puerto Rico, he was returning home to face choppy economic waters, which he tried to calm by preaching "mobilized voluntary action" as a cure-all for the Great Depression. Such rhetoric failed to impress millions of unemployed Americans who believed that the president was at best inept, at worst inhumane. His advisers urged him to demonstrate his humanity and searched for opportunities that would enable him to do so. Hoover listened because he wanted a second term.

The Denver Post for March 26, 1931, reported frigid temperatures in the city and even harsher weather outside of it. Still, the *Post* proclaimed "'Tis a Privilege to Live in Colorado." Frederick Bonfils, the paper's publisher, knew that his readers liked good news, heartthrob headlines, and sensationalism. On March 26 he gave them doses of each: a gangland story, reports of men getting drunk on radiator alcohol, the saga of a sleepwalking boy, and the marital woes of a would-be beauty queen. That he lived in one of the city's grandest mansions, that he was among Denver's richest men, and that his paper sold more than 300,000 copies each Sunday was not enough. Good stories made money. Bonfils wanted more.

On the eastern plains of Colorado that Thursday, twenty children—ordinary children who had likely never been in a mansion or seen a great ship except perhaps at a movie—struggled to keep from freezing to death in a stranded makeshift wooden school bus. Their lives and deaths (such good human stories) were soon caught in the webs spun by Frederick Bonfils and Herbert Hoover, who exploited the calamity without apparent concern for compounding it.

In *Children of the Storm: The True Story of the Pleasant Hill School Bus Tragedy*, Ariana Harner and Clark Secrest skillfully recount the Pleasant Hill disaster and its aftermath. Many details of the initial event have been told or mistold before. The scope of what happened afterward has not been related until now. Bonfils died in 1933, Hoover in 1964. Some of the survivors of the Pleasant Hill bus tragedy are still alive. Perhaps the truths brought out in *Children of the Storm* will help both the living and the dead rest in peace.

Stephen J. Leonard
Metropolitan State College, Denver
October 1999

Acknowledgments

THIS PROJECT BEGAN as a 1994 article in *Colorado Heritage*, the quarterly journal of the Colorado Historical Society. That article, prepared by editor Clark Secrest, was the result of interviews with three of the Pleasant Hill school bus tragedy survivors: Rosemary Brown Cannon, Blanche Stonebraker Widger, and Clara Smith Speer. In July 1997, Ariana Harner joined the Historical Society as an editorial assistant. Eventually, Harner and Secrest elected to collaborate on a further study of this misunderstood event.

The authors are grateful for the cooperation of numerous individuals. Each of the remaining survivors—Rosemary Brown Cannon, Maxine Brown Foreman, Alice Huffaker Huggins, Charley Huffaker, Laura Huffaker Loehr, Eunice Frost Youkey, and Blanche Stonebraker Widger—shared his or her often painful memories in at least one in-person interview and many follow-up calls. In addition, Georgene Pearson, Wanda Crum Maynard, Fern Reinert, and Lois McCracken related their knowledge of the event and its aftermath. Through Dr. Thomas Alby, superintendent of the Pueblo school district, the researchers contacted John L. Moser, who furnished basic biographical information about his mother, Maude Moser. In the search for information about Franz Freiday, Harner and Secrest are indebted to Joe Svoboda, Minnie Coonts, and James Franz Sherrill. Families of now-deceased survivors assisted the authors in understanding the event and aftermath: Margery Untiedt and children Judi, Linda, Teresa, and Jon discussed Bryan Untiedt's life; Ome Untiedt's widow, Faye, and daughter, Jo, talked about Ome's experiences; and Clara Smith Speer's son Darell generously shared his mother's memoirs and photographs. John Kenneth Herrick and Elbern Coons, Jr., recalled their experiences at the Reinert ranch, and Frances Marchbanks, the daughter of Dr. N. M. Burnett of the Charles Maxwell Hospital in Lamar, related knowledge of her father, who helped treat the frostbitten children.

Carol Garrett, registrar at the Colorado Department of Public Health, assisted in accessing the death certificate of Bobbie Brown. Colorado state archivist Terry Ketelsen and Erin McDanal of his staff located crucial school district records and correspondence. Special thanks go to Josephine Swenson of Lamar for furnishing photographs taken by J. H. Ward, who was among the first newsmen to reach the scene. Nadine Cheney of the Horace Greeley Museum in Tribune, Kansas, accessed her clippings collection for an important find. Joyce Huddleston, Greeley County assessor, pored through county clerk records for papers relating to 1933 legal actions resulting from the bus tragedy. Dr. Michael Yaron, associate professor of emergency medicine at the University of Colorado Health Sciences Center, offered revealing insight into the phenomenon of freezing to death, and hypothesized about the physical conditions of the Pleasant Hill children.

The authors express immense gratitude to their colleagues at the Colorado Historical Society. Librarians Rebecca Lintz and Barbara Dey assisted in the use of the library's microfilm holdings. Randy Swan shared his expertise about 1930s vehicles in helping formulate theories about the Pleasant Hill school bus. David N. Wetzel, director of publications, was supportive throughout, offering countless suggestions in strengthening this manuscript. The writers thank him for taking drafts home to edit and for mediating philosophical disagreements between the authors. Martha Dyckes, director of interpretive services, and Georgianna Contiguglia, president of the Colorado Historical Society, gave their blessings to this independent project.

Most profound appreciation goes to today's survivors of the Pleasant Hill bus tragedy. Hopefully, this book may finally close their wounds.

Notes to the Reader

THROUGH THE RECOLLECTIONS—some sixty-eight years after the event—of seven survivors and various key figures, and the thorough research of documents and extant newspaper clippings, the authors here attempt to accurately relate as many perspectives as research divulged. They have included aspects of this story that were previously untold or generally unknown. No dialogue, thoughts, or events have been manufactured or assumed.

The preponderance of information in this work comes from the Pleasant Hill survivors. Although individuals who lived through the tragedy were obviously able to provide the most accurate information about events on the bus, there were caveats. First, humans suffering physical and emotional shock are not in the ideal state to remember details. Second, the incident happened many years before the authors interviewed them, and time inevitably skews memory. Third, of the fifteen children who initially survived, only seven remained to be interviewed in 1998 and 1999. This story is a compilation of the recollections of these seven, with secondary information gleaned from friends and relatives of those directly involved, and archived records. A certain amount of skeptical credence was applied to journalistic accounts of the time.

Because the human memory is fallible and many years have passed, survivors' accounts differ in some instances. In such cases, the authors have identified commonalities among those individual memories and have noted the disagreements. Source citations, methodology notes, and discrepancies among survivors' memories can be found in the endnotes.

Specific points of view expressed in the narrative are directly attributed: "Rosemary Brown could not even see the radiator cap," for instance, comes directly from an interview with Rosemary Brown Cannon. A statement such as "Some parents were too proud to feel comfortable accepting gifts" indicates that at least two survivors indicated that general feeling. The sources of other such statements should be inherently clear in the text. For further information on sources and other published accounts, please refer to the bibliography.

Preface

IN 1931 LITTLE SLOWED the wind's sweep across Kiowa County's flat expanse of sagebrush, soapweed, low cactus, and the occasional wildflower mixed with the buffalo grass. Seldom a tree or farmstead interrupted the vast horizon of southeastern Colorado. Kiowa, the least populated of Colorado's southeastern counties, lacked timber, minerals, coal mining, industry, and water. Kiowa County's population stood at 3,786 (up only thirty-one people from ten years before), of which 518 resided in Eads, the county seat and only community of any size. The other 2,268 people were spread over the county's 1.1 million acres (1,720 square miles), or about one person for every 485 acres.

Virtually every family in Kiowa County was associated in some manner with dryland agriculture. Most of the county was given over to grain crops that required no irrigation; some parts had natural plains grasses, marginally suitable for grazing. On small dryland farms scattered throughout the countryside, hardworking people scratched out a living feeding livestock or chickens; raising small plots of alfalfa, corn, or wheat and selling their eggs, cream, grass, and grain. Sometimes crop yields could be traded for a used piece of farm machinery such as a tractor. The nearest marketing centers were Holly and Lamar, respectively seventeen and forty-nine miles to the south or southwest, in Prowers County. Lamar appropriately called itself the "capital" of southeastern Colorado, claiming 4,223 residents, banks, a railroad, a hospital, and even a dirt airstrip.

The Dust Bowl and Great Depression were still essentially two years into the future. Some Coloradans were optimistic, however, and believed that the ill economic winds blustering along the East Coast would never reach Colorado. In Kiowa County, land prices had always been low; some families even had been adding to their acreages by bringing in partners such as brothers, sisters, or parents.

Related families sometimes resided near each other and in that manner obtained assistance whenever necessary. In the district called Pleasant Hill, seventeen miles north of Holly, for instance, the interrelated Reinert, Frost, and Huffaker families farmed only a mile or two from each other. Similarly, Carl Miller, who supplemented his farm income by driving a school bus, had a brother and parents nearby to help out when needed. Family to family and neighbor to neighbor, everybody helped everybody else.

Fourteen miles north of Pleasant Hill on a seldom-traveled dirt road was the hamlet of Towner. From there, a traveler could proceed east two miles and be in Kansas, or forty-one miles west and be in Eads. Scattered among the farms were one-room schoolhouses that accommodated children from first through eighth grades. In many families, an education through eighth grade was considered adequate; no more than that was needed to help on the farm, and every hand was certainly needed. Families could be large—the Huffakers of Pleasant Hill, for instance, numbered nine, and all but the smallest child worked around the farm.

Washing was done on a washboard, and as many as four flat-irons were kept heating on the stove at one time. Water was carried by bucket from the well if a family were fortunate enough to have a well; otherwise it was hauled in five-gallon milk cans from a neighboring place. Farmer and school bus driver Carl Miller had a windmill-driven well. There, he filled a five-gallon milk can with water to carry over to the Pleasant Hill School (which had no other water supply for thirty students) on the running board of his bus each morning. Transporting water on the running boards of Model As or in the backs of wagons was a routine matter.

A barbed-wire fence lined the main road from Holly to Towner, but other than that, only an occasional farmstead broke the landscape. Homes were meager in their furnishings and fare. Rough boards often served as tables, and wooden crates as chairs. Ticking mattresses stuffed with straw or cornhusks—or maybe an occasional one stuffed with feathers—were placed on the floor or on a bunk for sleeping.

Sometimes houses were partially underground. These "dugouts" functioned like a basement with a roof and a stairwell. Inexpensive to construct, they were cool in the summer and held warmth in the winter—although just about every dugout leaked. Another potential problem was that during a blizzard, the snow could accumulate in the stairwell to the point that the people would have to exit through a window. A dugout could be used as a school, and some were walled up far enough to allow for a few windows. Elmer and Margaret Brown lived in a dugout just across the state line in Kansas, but sent their children to the Pleasant Hill School in Colorado because there was no school as close in Kansas.

One might believe that schools were few and far between, but they actually sprouted up about every ten miles because of the challenge of transporting children over long distances. When Kiowa County was formed in 1889, it had thirteen school districts but only two schoolhouses; the following year the county had twenty-three school districts and an equal number of schoolhouses. By 1931, the number of each was down to nineteen (with 1,360 students) including Pleasant Hill (with about thirty students). If a schoolhouse was no longer justified in a certain location, it was literally picked up and moved to where it would be more useful.

The opening of a new school was a significant community event. For instance, dedication of the new Towner School north of Pleasant

Hill featured a cornerstone ceremony, a baseball game, Stars-and-Stripes bunting, and a big welcome to folks from miles around. As well, a prayer and a cross burning followed a Ku Klux Klan parade, and in the evening a free picture show was projected onto a sheet strung between two trees.

Generally the conveyance to school was by a large car or, as in the case of Carl Miller, a makeshift bus body mounted on a truck bed. Schools were overseen by a teacher who instructed in the three Rs, history, geography, health, civics, and languages, plus honesty, independence, and integrity. Teachers generally boarded with a nearby family that had a student enrolled. Sometimes the teacher would move from family to family within the district. Because Pleasant Hill had two one-room schoolhouses—one for grades one through six and the other for seven and eight—it was unique in that it also had two teachers, Franz Freiday and Maude Moser. Because teachers were expected to arrive at school earlier than the students, Moser and Freiday drove their own cars to school each day.

The Pleasant Hill School began classes at 9:00 a.m. when Moser rang the handbell to call the students in from their games. (There was no playground equipment; the children of Pleasant Hill were fortunate just to have a few books to share.) Moser usually dismissed classes at 4:00 p.m. leaving blackboards to be cleaned, erasers to be dusted, and—in the winter—kindling and coal to be brought in for the next day.

On Sundays the school was sometimes used for worship. On Friday nights it served for community gatherings and potluck suppers, with games for the youngsters and conversations among adults. The school was also utilized for pie suppers, spelling and ciphering bees, literary evenings, and dances.

Few in these rural reaches yet had electricity by the early 1930s. Oil lamps and lanterns provided lighting, and a cellar—or "cave" as some people called it—served as refrigerator. Two multiparty phone circuits—the "Harmony Line" and the "Calamity Line"—had been strung along the fence post tops from Sheridan Lake and Towner to the Pleasant Hill district. Even at that, in 1931 the Stonebraker family had one of only a few telephones around. It worked surprisingly well when it was working, but it was usually broken when needed. Telephones were best used in emergencies because the rest of the time people used them for the purpose of gossiping. It was at least *something* to do; the radio stations broadcast from Pueblo were sometimes hard to hear. But when somebody needed to know the news, the radio—from Pueblo or even the powerful KOA in Denver, 175 air miles away—was depended upon for news bulletins. Occasionally somebody brought back from Holly a copy of *The Denver Post*, which was read closely by all members of the family even though its articles always appeared a bit sensational.

Pleasant Hill's gravel roads did not follow section lines, as they do today, and some of the roads weren't roads at all. Instead, residents took direct routes across the plains to the neighbor's house. For example, to get from the Pleasant Hill School to Andy Reinert's place, a diagonal route across the fields eliminated nearly a mile of travel.

If a family persevered and utilized hand-me-downs, it was possible to dress respectably despite the lack of wardrobe money. Little girls, for instance, might have worn flour-sack slips, but they generally had a few decent outer dresses to wear to school. And while the boys may have had mended and darned trousers, they were respectably washed and ironed. It was a matter of family pride. Occasionally a lucky Pleasant Hill schoolgirl might receive a store-bought warm sweater, which she would especially treasure when a chill blew across the uninterrupted plains.

This was the Pleasant Hill district upon which dawn broke on March 26, 1931. The events of the next thirty-three hours would horrify its people for a lifetime.

New Introduction
by the Authors

A TRIO OF FACTORS converged to bring about Southeast Colorado's Pleasant Hill school bus tragedy of 1931: a pair of decrepit, leaky, creaky wooden schoolhouses; a decrepit leaky, creaky wooden farm-truck-turned-school bus, and school administrators without a plan.

In the intervening years, thankfully, those factors have been reconsidered to ensure that a tragedy of this sort won't happen again. Ninety-three years have passed, but the memory of this event has become part of the fabric of the greater Holly area. Long gone are the paired ramshackle schoolhouses, replaced with a sturdy, two-story brick and metal structure near downtown Holly. The $22 million building, constructed in 2013 with a mix of local and governmental funding, is designed to resist all manner of hostile Eastern Plains weather. Under one roof, the building accommodates the entire Re-2 school district's 270 pupils, kindergarten through 12. Each grade has its own rooms, plus shared space: a gymnasium and critically, a kitchen. No blizzard can invade here. The structure is equipped even with tornado doors, which feature slide-bolt closures extending into concrete. In an emergency, this schoolhouse could shelter the town's seven hundred residents.

School leaders in today's Holly receive regular weather updates and have plans and procedures to meet any threats. In "awareness meetings," as Superintendent Charles Pollart terms them, school officials assess meteorological data received from the National Oceanic and Atmospheric Administration, beamed from facilities in Pueblo, and Dodge City, Kansas. Pollart—a Holly native whose family farm lies near the Pleasant Hill tragedy site—remarks that part of his staff's job is to "outguess" the weather, regardless of which not-in-frequent danger blows in. The community has survived tornados, severe dust storms, and blinding blizzards, and plans to continue to endure whatever weather the plains bring. Students will not be released under threatening circumstances; classes will be canceled proactively if danger looms.

Older pupils can drive themselves to school. When younger students do travel between school and home, they benefit from weatherproof buses built to federal standards to withstand extremes. The Holly school district runs five yellow buses over the district's 275 square miles, transporting about eighty students per day. Typical of many rural schools, classes are conducted Mondays through Thursdays to limit the time and cost of transportation. Each bus is equipped with a two-way radio. The school district shares a radio system with Prowers County but is working to obtain its own radio frequency and relay station. Each driver carries a cell phone as backup. Many drivers carry a stash of emergency snacks in the bus glove boxes. (Similarly, many private vehicles historically have carried emergency provisions during the winters, indicating how deeply the Pleasant Hill school bus tragedy is imprinted on the community.) Bus drivers are trained for weather emergencies and are personally acquainted with students and the families along their routes. Drivers conduct head counts on embarking and disembarking pupils.

Students travel and learn safely today largely thanks to technological improvements in meteorology, construction, and smart planning. But what makes the real difference is the community committed to remembering its history.

From our modern perspective nearly a century later, the hardworking people of Prowers and Kiowa counties in 1931 seemed pragmatic and communal and functional: neighbors knew each other and took care of each other's children and shared the little they had. That spirit saved the lives of twelve children. Yet even then, adults in power—from a media tycoon to a US president's public relations team—involved themselves to further their own agendas. The entire community found itself the center of international attention, and what group of regular folks, in 1931 or in 2024, is ever ready for that?

One of the most profoundly horrific human experiences, in any epoch, is losing a child. Technology may prevent foreseeable deaths, but it hasn't yet solved the challenges of getting through the day after such a loss. This story resonates today because children are still vulnerable and dependent on adults. The children of this storm wrestled their whole lives with the complexities of heroism or feeling responsible for the deaths of younger children.

Ariana Harner and Clark Secrest
August 2024

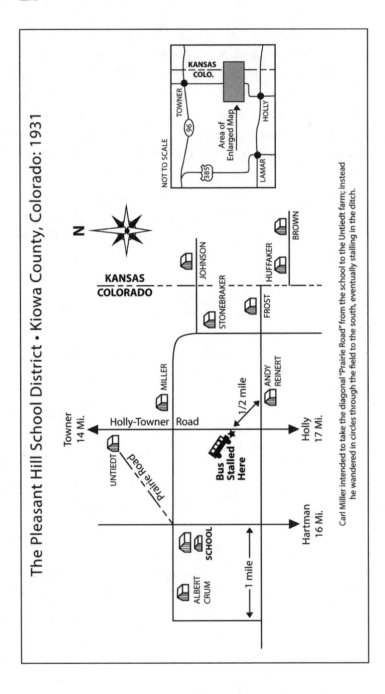

The Pleasant Hill School District • Kiowa County, Colorado: 1931

Carl Miller intended to take the diagonal "Prairie Road" from the school to the Untiedt farm; instead he wandered in circles through the field to the south, eventually stalling in the ditch.

CHAPTER ONE

The Children
of Pleasant Hill

THE RISING SUN illuminated Kansas, and light crept across the plains of southeastern Colorado. It was now the end of March, and winter-weary families hoped the winds were gone that had scooped up and flung the snow and cold from farm to farm. The vicissitudes of the weather ruled these hardy people; during winter, they often were unable to journey by car or horse even to Holly, the nearest town. And although the Great Depression had not yet affected these poor ranchers and farmers, the forthcoming summer would bring the first of many droughts that would dry the earth and dogged winds that would rip topsoil from the farms.

On the remote plains this morning of March 26, 1931, low clouds extended from horizon to horizon, and the air was an uncommonly warm sixty degrees. The people were relieved. The troubles of winter were gone for another year.

Carl and Geneva Miller woke early to tend to their children—Louis, eighteen months, and Mary Louise, age eight—and to feed the cattle in the barn. When Geneva came into Mary Louise's room to wake her for school, the little girl pushed aside the flour-sack curtain and peered out over the flatness. A few trees and tiny adobe-and-frame farmhouses dotted the dawning landscape. What a beautiful day it promised to be! Mary Louise decided that when she returned home from school that afternoon, she would take her pony, Prince, for a ride. Though she was only in the third grade, she knew how to saddle Prince herself. She looked forward to the hour or so each afternoon when she was not needed to help with chores and could gallop across the plains toward the horizon. In the mornings, however, Mary Louise was obligated to get dressed and help her mother prepare breakfast.

Like many other Americans of 1931, the Millers were poor but resourceful. They had moved from Kansas to be near Carl's parents and brother, and felt fortunate to have found 160 acres to lease. In addition to cultivating crops and raising chickens, pigs, and cattle, Miller received $100 a month from the school board to transport the children of eastern Kiowa County to the Pleasant Hill School—two wood-frame buildings about a mile and a half west of the Miller place. Schoolhouses were scattered in small intervals across the plains, affording every child an opportunity for an education through the eighth grade. Those wishing to complete high school had to board in Holly and attend the school there.

Miller's 1929 Chevrolet farm truck had been fitted with a dusky-blue, wooden school bus body that had five windows along each side. He welcomed the additional money he earned from transporting youngsters to the Pleasant Hill School, and because he had always been skilled at fixing farm equipment, he had no cause for worry whenever the vehicle might break down. During summer vacation, Miller utilized the truck bed, without its bus top, in the fields. When the autumn harvest was at its peak and Carl and his brother worked long hours bringing in the crops, Geneva would bundle up little Louis and save Carl several hours of work by driving the school bus route herself.

At 7:20 a.m. Miller stepped from the back of the farmhouse and out of habit grabbed his fur-lined overcoat hanging next to the door, above the washtubs. He called to Mary Louise, who was washing dishes, that he would return in the bus to get her in about an hour. It usually took him at least an hour, depending on the weather, to pick up the twenty or so young people on his school bus route and deliver them to the Pleasant Hill School. Geneva was in the barn milking; he would help when he returned.

Transporting water for the students was also a part of Miller's job because the school had no well. On this particular morning he dipped the bucket into the windmill tank, then glanced at the sky— so vast it seemed he could almost see the curvature of the earth. By the time he filled the water can and looked up again, the sun no longer shone yellow but was turning amber on the horizon. The sky momentarily seemed odd, Miller expected a bluer sky—but never mind. What a relief that spring, the most welcome season, would be along in the next few weeks. With spring, color would tinge the normally bleak landscape: buffalo grass, now dormant and brown, soon would be a green haze stretching to the horizon in every direction; placid brown and white cattle would begin grazing; the sky would grow tall and become intensely blue; and buds would form on the tips of the occasional tree. Miller looked forward to the upcoming weeks. Now, though, he saw only brown and gray—nude trees, bare earth, gravel and dirt roads, and adobe-brick walls.

Miller entered the bus to readjust the piece of cardboard in one of the back windows. If he could ever get extra cash (an unlikely thought), he planned to replace the broken-out glass in the bus's two rear windows. For now, he made do with cardboard inserted into the frames.

The air was so warm! He considered leaving his overcoat at home but decided not to take the time. He certainly would not need it this balmy morning. Miller cranked up the engine and chugged off on his morning rounds to the Pleasant Hill School. It was 7:30 a.m.; he was right on time. He would be back on the farm by 9:00 a.m. for his chores.

The family of Elmer and Margaret Brown lived in a two-room dugout a few hundred yards into Kansas, across the Colorado state line. Little more than a large, covered hole, the home consisted of a kitchen and one bedroom for the family of seven. Rosemary, age thirteen; Bobbie, eleven; and Maxine, eight, looked forward to escaping from their cramped underground home to join their friends at the Pleasant Hill School. Because they lived farthest from the school, Miller picked up the Brown youngsters first, then worked his way back toward Pleasant Hill, three and a half miles northwest. It was the Browns' first year living here; Elmer farmed and ranched a rented 640 acres that was close enough to Holly (nineteen miles south) that he could exchange his cream and eggs for grocery staples at the general store. Though the Brown farm was officially situated in Greeley County, Kansas, the Pleasant Hill School was closer than the nearest Kansas school; therefore, Greeley County paid Kiowa County for educating the three youngest Brown children. (Harold and Roy, the elder children, had completed school through ninth grade and now helped their father on the farm.)

While Bobbie Brown slopped the hogs as he did every morning, his mother, Margaret, called out to remind him to take a coat in case a wind came up. Just then, the bus arrived, and no time remained to dart into the house for his jacket. Bobbie threw down the bucket and ran to the bus. His sisters, Rosemary and Maxine, emerged from the house where they had been helping clean up the breakfast dishes and make beds. They took the coats their mother handed them and put them on as they ran down the path. They wondered why; it was so warm. Maxine waved goodbye to their German shepherd, Fritz.

The Browns' closest neighbors were Bessie and Reuben Huffaker, who also lived just into Kansas. There, the six school-age Huffaker children clambered aboard Miller's Chevrolet: Alice, age fourteen; Charley, twelve; Carl, eleven; Max, ten; Lena, nine; and Laura, seven. Baby Betty and Robert, not yet old enough for school, and Gladys, who had already completed junior high, stayed at home. Though the Browns and Huffakers lived only a half mile apart, the youngsters were kept so busy on their farms that the school bus and the schoolhouse provided the only regular opportunities for socializing. Every morning Charley Huffaker milked the cows and fed the hogs. Alice was responsible for making sure her younger siblings made their beds before she went out to the barn to milk her five cows. Bessie, their mother, insisted that the entire family sit down to a hearty breakfast each morning, and the girls, even little Laura, helped prepare the meal. Then Bessie packed their lunches with beef or pork sandwiches and, in the autumn, if not too expensive, apples. Sometimes it grew tiresome to eat the same foods day after day, but Alice secretly traded with her friend Eunice Frost, who wearied of her own usual peanut butter sandwich. None of the Huffaker children dared complain that almost every wintertime supper consisted of cornbread and milk because they knew they were luckier than many families. They lived in a dugout house with an adobe ground-level addition, and their father, Reuben, owned four hundred acres, a new car, and—unlike most farmers—owed no debts. Nobody in the Huffaker family went hungry or wore shoddy clothes, and even on a morning as warm as this, their mother insisted they bundle up.

With six of her children now safely aboard Carl Miller's bus and off to the Pleasant Hill School for the day, Bessie Huffaker turned on the radio to hear the weather report from Pueblo. It called for snow! How odd on a day promising such warmth. Of course the weatherman probably confined the forecast to Pueblo, 170 miles to the west, and certainly could not mean the Holly area. She glanced at the sky, noticing dark clouds gathering over the northern horizon—perhaps the weatherman was correct after all. Spring snowstorms on these plains could drop a good measure of snow but were quick to melt, nurturing the winter wheat and corn. Plus, spring storms never got very cold. Whatever was coming would probably blow over, Bessie

Huffaker thought as she began gathering up dirty clothing and calming the baby. Today was washday, and she had better get started by boiling water.

In the Claude Frost household, a quarter mile northwest of the Huffakers and just inside Colorado, Eunice, fourteen, and Leland, seven, hurried to get ready for school. They washed their necks and ears (always ordered by their mother, Mary Muriel), combed their hair, brushed their teeth, gulped breakfast, then grabbed wraps and lunchpails, and scampered out to meet Carl Miller's approaching bus. Their mother called to them to put on warmer clothes despite the balmy temperature, so Eunice dashed back into the house for her four-buckle overshoes. Ever protective of her happy-go-lucky younger brother, Leland, Eunice clutched his hand to help him climb onto the Chevrolet's running board. She greeted her cousins, the Huffaker children.

Louise and Blanche Stonebraker lived with their parents, Dave and Nellie, nearly a mile north of the Frosts. As the bus rumbled into view along the gravel road toward the Stonebraker place, Louise was bickering with her mother. For her upcoming fourteenth birthday, only five days away, Louise had received a cardigan sweater, and she begged to wear it to school. Nellie Stonebraker demanded that she put on a coat instead, but Louise argued that the sweater was heavy enough on a day as warm as this. The ride to school was not very long, anyway! In exasperation her mother relented, and Louise strode toward the bus in her new cardigan. Ten-year-old Blanche ran ahead to sit with her friends Maxine Brown and Lena and Laura Huffaker.

Bus driver Carl Miller studied the sky again. The clouds, no longer lying on the horizon, puffed high in the sky, tinged with amber from the blowing dust. Clouds roiled from dark blue to light blue and back to dark blue, a phenomenon foreign to Miller. Certainly, the day had begun warm. Now the western horizon was darkening and a chill was coming. He had hoped to plow the garden after delivering his charges; however, if a storm were brewing, he might have to wait a day or two.

The bus drove on toward the two-story stucco farmhouse of Ernie and Florence Johnson to pick up their adopted child, Kenneth, age seven. That done, Carl Miller followed the turn in the road west to his own home, where chickens scurried about the yard. He honked the horn and his daughter, Mary Louise, ran out with her open coat flapping. It was 8:20 a.m.; he was right on time.

Usually, Miller picked up five children at his next stop, the Untiedt (pronounced "Unteed") place. For the last several weeks, however, fourteen-year-old Clara Smith had been living with the family of Bud and Hazel Untiedt in exchange for helping Hazel with the children and house chores, bringing the total to six. Because she was shy, Clara found it difficult to live with someone else's large family, but it was necessary, and she liked the Untiedts. Clara's own family had recently rented a farm near Hartman, about six miles northwest of Holly, but she wanted to finish the school year at the Pleasant Hill School before joining them. (Her sister, Nora, was living with the Albert Crum family nearby for the same reason.) This was, after all, her final year before high school, as she planned, unlike many farm children, to continue her schooling through the twelfth grade. She would attend high school in Holly the following year, where she would again have to room. The current arrangements for Clara and Nora helped ease the financial burden on the Smith family.

As the bus bumped toward the Untiedt place, Clara hurried to help Hazel clean up the breakfast dishes of the five children, ages eight to twelve. Virgil Untiedt, age eleven, was recovering from a recent burn accident, so he remained home. Bryan, at twelve, the eldest of the Untiedt children and tall for his age, kissed baby Ruth Elaine (he loved children), then ducked through the door to catch the bus. Bryan got along well with the younger ones and was always eager to join them on the bus. His ten-year-old sister, Evelyn, grabbed her lunch bucket and ran to catch up with Bryan and brothers Ome, nine, and Arlo, eight. (They called Evelyn "Tommie" because she was a *girl* rather than one of them, but they liked her anyway.) Ome and Arlo, who resembled each other in appearance and in personality, scurried in tandem to the bus. Clara Smith draped her light coat across her shoulders and joined the group hurrying for the bus. The sky looked the way it did when a snowstorm was approaching, and the chill was intensifying. *What happened to the nice morning?* Clara wondered. She knew that March snowstorms in Colorado could dump a lot of wet snow, but that it never got very cold and the snow would melt in a day or two. This would probably blow over.

❄✳❄✳❄

Carl Miller was one of two school bus drivers in the Pleasant Hill district. He picked up the children who lived on the eastern half, while the seven students who lived on the western half rode in an auto driven by Oscar Reinert. Reinert's route took him only forty-five minutes.

Unlike Miller, Reinert had lived in Kiowa County his whole life and knew the ways of the eastern Colorado plains. On this morning, the dark clouds and quickening breeze from the north worried him. It was only 8:30 a.m.; Reinert would probably have time to return his charges to their homes if a storm were to blow in suddenly.

One of Reinert's passengers, ten-year-old Wanda Crum, was particularly looking forward to seeing her best friend, Evelyn Untiedt, who was on Carl Miller's bus. School would only last another six weeks, and then they would be off for the summer to work on their farms. Though Wanda lived only two miles across the fields from the Untiedts, she and Evelyn were not able to pal around during the summer; their parents had no time to transport each to the other's home, and there was always work to be done. Every child living on a farm contributed to the workload; youth or a diminutive physique was not an excuse for sloth.

Fifteen-year-old Nora Smith, another of Reinert's passengers, anticipated seeing her sister, Clara, at school. While Clara worked as a house girl in the Untiedt home, Nora stayed with Albert and Erma Crum, relatives of young Wanda Crum, and helped take care of their baby, Clifford. Nora and Clara enjoyed staying with these families, but as the only girls in their family of seven children, they were very close and missed living together. At least they still saw each other at school.

Teacher Maude Moser departed for school as the air was beginning to chill. She was accustomed to the occasionally harsh weather of southeastern Colorado.[1] Except for her four years of study at the Colorado State College of Education in Greeley and two years of teaching in the Pueblo area, Moser had lived in this area her entire life. Her husband, George, resided with his brother thirty-three miles northeast in Tribune, Kansas. During their seven years of marriage, they had only lived together during summer vacations and visited on weekends. Economy forced them to reside wherever jobs were available, which currently meant living apart. George found work in Tribune at a small mill, and Maude's position as a teacher in the Pleasant Hill district required her to board nearby. So she resided with August Reinert (west-side driver Oscar Reinert's father) a mile south of the twin Pleasant Hill schoolhouses.

Moser shared teaching responsibilities with twenty-three-year-old Franz Freiday. Freiday had received his necessary professional credits and teaching certificate in Park County in 1930. This job marked the first year of teaching for the Rising City, Nebraska, native. For individual salaries of $945 for the nine-month school year, each was expected to teach classes, monitor the students during recess and lunch, accompany the little ones to the outdoor privy, keep the building and grounds clean and neat, communicate with the two bus drivers, and in the winter, keep fires going in the sheet-steel coal stoves.

By the time Moser reached the schoolyard at 8:50 a.m., the sky was foreboding. She checked the supply of coal in the shed; a new load had been delivered recently so that, even if the air suddenly turned cold, there would be enough to keep the schoolhouses warm. The sound of a car engine signaled Freiday's arrival.[2]

The pair of one-room, detached structures constituting the Pleasant Hill School was neither pleasant nor on a hill. The lonesome buildings were isolated from everything but the elements. A barbed-wire fence enclosed the property, and two outhouses stood about fifty feet behind the elementary school building. No trees grew in the schoolyard; indeed, vegetation was sparse across the horizon. The closest farmhouse was a half mile west, sheltered only by the rarity of a clump of trees.

Maude Moser taught grades one through six in the north building, which had four windows and a tacked-on shed with a lean-to roof. The building to the south—the smaller one with three windows on each side and a similarly attached shed—was where Freiday taught the seventh- and eighth-grade students.[3] The frame buildings were in poor condition; even the Kiowa County school superintendent's 1930–1931 annual report admitted as much. Nonetheless, the school buildings served additionally as this farm community's primary meeting place. A Sunday school class, public meeting, or occasional summer picnic allowed the isolated families to socialize.

Moser's elementary school building contained enough wooden desks with flip-up seats for thirty children. The younger students sat up front; the fifth and sixth graders were in the back. The blackboard stretched across the front of the room behind Moser's plain-and-sturdy block of an oak desk. She kept her desk clear except for the small bell that she used to call the youngsters in from the playground, which was between the buildings. The cylindrical coal stove, tucked into a corner, stood as tall as Moser and radiated steady heat—necessary to combat the winds that seeped through the window frames. A stand next to the door held a washbasin. A tin cup hung from a peg, and a flour-sack towel was draped over the side of the washstand. The piano in the front, though out of tune, provided music for singing hymns during Sunday school and for the school Christmas pageant. Bessie Huffaker, who played piano better than anyone else in eastern Kiowa County, usually led the songs.

Outside, the wind was already whistling at the schoolhouse windows. The sky darkened and a few flakes of snow swirled about as Carl Miller's wooden bus bumped across the barrow pit and into the schoolyard with its twenty chattering passengers. Moser opened her building's door to find Freiday walking across the yard toward her. They apprehensively scanned the north sky, which now held monstrous-looking clouds. The teachers knew that dust, wind, and cold blew indiscriminately through cracks in the thin wooden walls of the schoolhouses, as well as through the window frames. If this weather were to worsen into a storm, the buildings would be drafty and chilly—especially if they all had to remain overnight. Besides, Moser and Freiday reasoned to each other, the children brought only enough food for lunch. There were no beds or blankets, of course, and the drinking and washing water that Carl Miller hauled every morning from his well to the school might not be enough to last through the night. Additionally, the teachers might not have relished being cooped up with twenty-seven rambunctious schoolchildren.

The youngsters piled off the bus, pulling wraps around their bodies against the chill. Some began chasing each other across the dirt yard (now dusted with fluffy snowflakes) in a game they called "fox and geese," waiting for their classmates from the west side to arrive in Oscar Reinert's car.

Alice Huffaker and the other older children left the younger ones frolicking and laughing in the snow and followed Carl Miller inside the larger school building while some of the older boys took the empty buckets to the coal shed to fill. A sudden gust of wind slammed the door shut behind them. Freiday and Moser summoned Miller and suggested it would be better for everyone if he returned the children home immediately, rather than waiting until the storm passed. Even if the storm became violent before he delivered them all, they would be safe at one of the nearby farmhouses, where they would be able to eat, stay warm, and even sleep if the storm lasted through the night. (In this desolate farming community, neighbors and strangers helped each other all the time.) This schoolhouse was inadequate, the teachers told Miller, for twenty-seven children and four adults to remain comfortably through a bad storm. Miller disagreed: In the hour and a half it took him to pick up all the children, the temperature had dropped at least ten degrees and the clouds had rolled in faster than his bus could travel. And now! He gestured at the thickening snowfall and gray sky. At least, Miller argued, there was a stove in the schoolhouse and they could stay warm. And the storm would probably pass over quickly, as spring snowstorms in this part of the country usually did. Some of the parents, Miller added, might even come to the school to pick up their children once the weather cleared. They would expect to find their children here, not someplace else, he insisted.

Freiday and Moser remained adamant that Miller should take the youngsters away.[4] Miller, they said, could be at the Untiedt house in a few minutes, before the storm worsened. One rear wheel of the bus remained equipped with its winter snow and mud chains, and Miller could easily beat the oncoming storm if he left right away.

So before the young people had time to remove their coats, the teachers announced that Miller would take them to the nearest farm-

This interior view of the elementary classroom the year after the tragedy shows Ome Untiedt (front, far left row); Laura Huffaker (front, second row); Blanche Stonebraker (behind Laura); Leland Frost (front, third row); Carl Huffaker (two desks behind Leland); and Max Huffaker (back, fourth row). The new teacher is Louise Binder.

house—or to their own homes if the weather did not worsen—while they remained at the school to wait for Oscar Reinert's west-side car.

Moser, seeing that Laura Huffaker's hat had fallen askew, replaced it and tied it under her chin. Then the teacher smiled and told the children to button their coats. As Miller strode from the school, Blanche Stonebraker noticed him wipe away an angry tear.

Excited at the prospect of an unexpected holiday, the youngsters rushed across the schoolyard toward the wooden bus with the cardboard windows. The north wind was gathering force, and the older students steadied the younger and smaller ones against the gale. Laura clutched her newly tightened hat strings. The snow thickened—so heavy now that the children had to concentrate to see each other clearly. What a drastic change from just an hour ago—indeed, from mere minutes ago. What happened to springtime?

Two parallel wooden benches lined the bus compartment, beneath which the children stowed their metal lunchpails. As usual, Laura Huffaker tried not to kick hers with her dangling feet. She faced Evelyn Untiedt, who sat across the three-foot aisle. Rosemary Brown took the place behind the driver.

It was 9:00 a.m. Miller started the engine, and the bus lurched from the schoolyard onto the gravel road in a blinding swirl of snow. The relieved teachers watched the vehicle disappear into the whiteness. By the time the bus reached the road, the children could no longer see the school. Carl Miller could not see the radiator cap on his hood. Instantly, he was lost.

CHAPTER TWO

Lost

IN HIS CONFUSION, Carl Miller turned east on the east-west road, instead of following the diagonal ruts northeast across the prairie leading directly to the Untiedt place. Charley Huffaker, Clara Smith, and Rosemary Brown could not determine which direction Miller was driving; they assumed he must be taking the usual shortcut to the Untiedt home. Blanche Stonebraker, only ten years old, knew the route was not typical but did not feel alarmed.

Charley wondered to himself how Miller could possibly see the road or where he was going, as none of the children could detect anything but snow. Why, when Miller had been reluctant to depart into the storm, did he not return to the schoolyard? Still, the young passengers in their flimsy capsule were not worried as the bus lurched into the maelstrom; after all, it was a serendipitous vacation from arithmetic and spelling lessons. Someone started singing the popular tune "Old Black Joe," and everybody joined in:

> Gone are the days when our hearts were young and gay;
> Gone are our friends from the cotton fields away.
> Grieving for friends now departed long ago;
> I hear their gentle voices calling,
> "Old Black Joe."

Back at the Pleasant Hill School, Maude Moser and Franz Freiday discussed their options. Moser felt confident that she could return south to August Reinert's place. Freiday watched her drive away; the wind seemed to be lessening. But Freiday, who lived farther away, thought it would be prudent to wait out the storm.

Miller opened the driver-side window and put his head outside the bus in an attempt to discern a landmark, or even whether he was on a road, which was uncertain. The older children were beginning to suspect that Miller was no longer on the road but was perhaps meandering southward across fields. Miller leaned back toward Rosemary Brown and asked if she could see anything. She could not, but she did notice tiny slivers of ice on Miller's eyelashes and frozen droplets on his cheeks. Eunice Frost, farther toward the back, caught Rosemary's glance. Even if their younger siblings and classmates did not realize it, thirteen-year-old Rosemary and fourteen-year-old Eunice knew they were potentially in danger. Clara Smith—at nearly fifteen, the oldest pupil on the bus—knew for certain of their troubling predicament as the little bus plowed blindly onward.

Keep singing, they thought. *At least we can keep the little ones from worrying.* Only a quarter-mile to the west of Miller's bus, Oscar Reinert, in his car full of young people, knew from the wind's behavior and the manner in which it buffeted the snow that this could be a severe plains blizzard. He didn't trust these circumstances. Suddenly, Reinert was able to discern a small house. He stopped the car and knocked on the door. Albert Crum, a second cousin of ten-year-old Wanda Crum, urged the travelers inside. *Safe.*

Miller, trying the best he could, blundered on through the white flatness, hoping to pick up a road, fence—something—to establish his location.[5] He could not know in his growing confusion that he was getting farther and farther from the road. Even from her position halfway down the bus, Eunice Frost saw that the windshield was now frozen over, opaque. Miller again thrust his head through the side window into the blizzard, hoping to see something, anything at all; but it only served to let the ferocious wind and snow into the bus. Clara Smith guessed that they had been gone from the school for fifteen minutes. Alice Huffaker wondered why there was no heater on the bus. It was growing cold. Her younger sister Lena was robust and seemed comfortable, but little Laura Huffaker, the youngest child on the bus, was starting to shiver. Alice looked around at the singing crowd. White clouds flew from their mouths as they sang.

The wind tore at the flimsy cardboard covering the two broken windows at the rear of the bus. Clara Smith tugged her collar higher against the draft, hoping they soon would be romping around inside the Untiedts' warm house. Laura Huffaker was suddenly grateful for her hat with the earflaps that Maude Moser had tied snugly under her chin. Louise Stonebraker would never have wanted to admit to her mother that perhaps she should have worn a coat instead of her knitted birthday sweater.

The bus bumped its way into blankness; its youngest passengers, in their youthful naivete, were safe in their belief that nothing bad could ever happen to them. Evelyn Untiedt argued playfully with the younger children about whose skills at schoolyard games were superior and whose pets were the most fun. Having this unexpected day off was certainly lucky!

Carl Miller pulled out his pocket watch. It was 9:30 a.m. He knew that even in this weather, the bus should have reached some ranch fifteen minutes ago. Miller returned the watch to the pocket of his overalls and rolled up his window. *Just keep driving. Eventually we will hit a road.* The gusting snow cloaked the bus in flat whiteness.

Suddenly, the front wheels dipped, then climbed up. A road-side barrow ditch! As the front wheels bounced onto the ice-coated gravel, the back wheels spun—even the tire chains were unable to push the bus up the ditch's slope.

"*Gone are the days when our hearts were young and . . .*"

The Pleasant Hill bus jolted sharply and the singing stopped. The engine coughed, then died.

The storm shrieked on.

CHAPTER THREE

The First Day

AFTER A MOMENTARY STILLNESS, the wind resumed. Carl Miller took a deep breath and tried to restart the engine. Nothing happened. He tried again, then announced he would go outside to check the engine's wiring. Miller felt his way to the front of the vehicle and lifted the hood, but the wires were soaked, preventing the spark plugs from firing. Miller made his way around back and recognized that even if the engine could start, the only chains, on the right wheel, were useless against the angle of the ditch. Beyond his outstretched hand, Miller could see only white.

The children of Pleasant Hill were trapped in the most widespread blizzard to hit Colorado in fifty-six years, and it was *cold*, unlike most spring storms. The youngsters could not know that even 252 miles northwest, in the capital city of Denver, and beyond, wind swirled snow around ceaselessly, downing telegraph lines and blocking train tracks. Statewide storms of this magnitude were rare in Colorado, and this blizzard extended even beyond the state's boundaries: Before it ended, herds of cattle from Idaho to the panhandle of Oklahoma would freeze to death or suffocate from the snow clogging their nostrils. Children were trapped in their schoolhouses elsewhere in Colorado and in Kansas, but on the flatness of Pleasant Hill, there were twenty children marooned in a drafty school bus with wet cardboard window replacements that were now flapping at the edges, and temperatures that would continue to drop for another twenty-four hours.

After his fruitless attempt to restart the engine, Carl Miller recognized the peril. He summoned Bryan Untiedt, the oldest boy, to help him drain the radiator so it would not freeze. When they returned, they were grateful that although the interior was little warmer than the outdoors, most of the wind's violence was kept outside. The cold seeped in through the floorboards and the gaps in the wall joints.

Perhaps a fire would keep everyone warm for a while. Trying to be cheerful, Miller rallied the children to help him gather fuel from within the bus. He retrieved the milk can lid from the bus's running board and placed it in the aisle between the facing wood benches.[6] Children handed him pages from their notebooks and textbooks. Someone pried shards of wood from the driver's splintered seat.

Miller lighted the wood and paper, but the flame was small and the paper, taken from small damp hands, would not burn. Acrid smoke billowed up and filled the bus interior, and the youngsters coughed. They reopened the driver-side window to let the smoke out. Rosemary Brown, for one, preferred the penetrating cold to the smoke. And besides, how large of a fire could a can lid contain? Certainly not enough to make a difference in the growing cold.

Miller knew he must keep the children moving to fight off sleep. He widened the aisle one foot by shoving the benches flush against the walls. He told the young people to hop up and down, wave their arms, and mock fight each other. They had set out from the school two hours earlier; *surely* the storm would ease up before supper. The younger children, who in their naivete still believed it all to be just an adventure, happily followed his instructions.

The snow swirled ruthlessly around the lonely bus—a wooden box on wheels, a mere speck in the blizzard. No other human beings knew it was there, lost and motionless. Untold millions of tiny particles of frozen water held it captive—life-sustaining water, sometimes scant on this semiarid prairie. Now in its solid form, that same sustenance threatened the lives of twenty-one people.

The cardboard pieces covering the two broken rear-side windows were becoming increasingly flimsy from the relentless wind and wet snow. Suddenly the wind tore one from the window frame and flung it onto the wooden floor. The gale blasted through the opening, and snow hurled inside.[7] Miller shouted over the noise of the wind that the youngsters *must keep moving! Keep moving, no matter what!*

❄❆❄❆❄

One mile northwest, inside the cozy two-room Crum residence, Erma Crum heated water for her family and the eight unexpected guests they were sheltering from the storm. She was worried about the pantry. If the children must stay overnight, she knew the scant food supply would soon be gone—as would the fuel. The family had not been to the market in Holly recently, and in these past few lean years, the grocery store's stock had often been short. Hopefully, the storm would clear in time for the youngsters to be delivered home by evening. In the meantime, Erma, with Nora Smith's help, could fix hot coffee for the children to drink while they ate the lunches they had brought from home. So far, the youngsters appeared to be having fun, laughing and playing in the next room. As the storm worsened, some wondered where the children from the east-side bus were—safe in the Pleasant Hill schoolhouses, they assumed.

Yet no children played in those schoolhouses. Instead, teacher Franz Freiday now huddled alone at the stove, preparing to settle in for as many hours as it would take for the storm to blow over.

He had started his Ford and traveled about a hundred yards north-west before it got stuck. Knowing there was coal in the schoolhouse, Freiday struggled back on foot, fortunate to find the fence that surrounded the schoolyard. Blowing snow stung his face and blocked his vision. He grabbed the wire and proceeded hand-over-hand until he reached the gate, then he headed straight for the larger schoolhouse. He hoped that Maude Moser had made it home.[8]

Bobbie Brown no longer thought that jumping around in Carl Miller's makeshift school bus was fun. He was hungry. His sister Maxine realized as much and leaned down to retrieve her lunch-pail from beneath the bench. That's when she noticed—everyone noticed—that the snow blowing into the bus had packed around the pails, freezing them solid to the floor. The children tried to kick them loose, but it was no use—a block of packed snow and ice encased their only food. Even the lids, frozen to the pails, could not be pried open. Suddenly realizing they were without food, everyone felt the oncoming hunger.

Although the stranded schoolchildren did not discuss their thoughts, the six Huffakers remembered that this was Thursday—not only washday at their household, but also one of the days their mother baked bread. While the clothes and bedclothes boiled in the copper washtub on the stove, Bessie Huffaker mixed dough and kneaded ten loaves of bread. After setting the bread on the kitchen table to cool, she used the still-hot oven to bake cookies. Every Thursday, when the bus returned the small Huffakers to their home, the aroma of warm fresh bread and cookies would greet them at the door. Each was allowed one cookie, but that was the only snack until dinner. Trapped in Carl Miller's freezing bus, enveloped by whiteness, the Huffaker children were smelling that kitchen aroma, tasting those warm, sweet cookies, and knowing that somebody would come get them soon and take them home.

The wind howled louder and rocked the wooden bus; the temperature dropped. Laura Huffaker, sitting on her sister Alice's lap, whispered that she needed to go to the bathroom. Alice told her to go in her underpants, as the heat, at least, would keep her skin warm for a while.[9]

"Exercise, everyone!" Miller commanded again, and the children dutifully arose and jogged in place. Laura's underpants were no longer warm. In fact, the chilly wind blew through the soggy fabric worse than if it had been dry. She tugged on her coat, but it was too short to cover her rear. She begged Alice to let her sit on her lap again, and her sister relented. Others kept moving about. At Miller's counsel, they all bellowed together for help. None came.

Carl Miller checked his pocket watch. It was 3:00 p.m. The smaller children had been as obedient and patient as could be expected, and they were wearying of it. Miller told the older children to choose a younger one to pay particular attention to: slap him, shake her, keep them moving! If anyone were to sit down and doze off . . . he refused to think of that. Reluctantly, they kept moving. They were so many children in such a small space that they bumped into each other by accident and boxed at one another on purpose. Evelyn Untiedt briefly contemplated her peanut butter sandwich trapped in a block of ice under the bench. If she were at home right now, she would bask in front of the coal cookstove and toast her feet by the open oven.

Miller selected the oldest boy and girl, Bryan Untiedt and Clara Smith, to leave the bus and search for a fence. Maybe that would help them figure out where they were, and they could seek help by following the fence line to a house. Seeing that Bryan was wearing only a light coat and sweater, Miller gave Bryan his own sheepskin-lined coat to wear during the search. When Miller opened the door, stinging snow rushed in. Clara and Bryan, their bodies bent into the gale, struggled to stay upright, let alone locate a fence line. After a few feet, they turned and looked back toward the bus, a shimmering dark shape visible only when they squinted against the bright snow. Just then, Bryan stumbled and fell. It seemed to Clara a long time before she was able to fight the wind to help him up. They started off again, but Clara lost her balance and he had to pull her up. They staggered on slowly. The sensation in their legs was diminishing, until it felt as if they were walking on wooden pegs. Bryan fell again and Clara kept walking. He shouted for her to help him, but she stalled, fearing that if she fell she would not be able to stand again. When he called to her a second time, she knew he could not get up without her help, so she turned back. Progress through the whiteness was difficult to gauge because she could not feel her feet. She reached out to Bryan and he rose stiffly. They held tightly to each other's gloved hands, slowly returning to the bus. Once there, they were so weak and breathless they could only scratch their hands on the door to get the attention of the children inside. The door opened, and they lifted their feet onto the running board, then tumbled inside.

The other children rubbed Clara's and Bryan's legs until the feeling returned. Clara now felt so sleepy that she wanted to curl up for a nap, but the others slapped and shook her alert. The older children—Rosemary Brown, Eunice Frost, Clara Smith, Bryan Untiedt, Louise Stonebraker, and Charley and Alice Huffaker—knew the busload of children faced danger. Clara told them that she and Bryan had been unable to locate any sort of marker. They knew no more than they had before going into the storm.

Eunice Frost wondered how this bus could possibly get any colder. She did not need a thermometer to know that the temperature was declining steadily, maybe to zero by now. All she knew was that she was terribly cold, the coldest she had ever been. Exercising was not helping her warm up, but it was the only option at this point. She looked for her friend Louise Stonebraker, but did not see Louise's head among those bobbing wearily up and down. Finally, she located Louise at the back of the bus, sitting on the bench as far to the rear as possible, at the edge of the chaos of the wildly exercising children. Louise must have been sitting there the entire time! Jostling her way to the back, Eunice asked why Louise would not exercise—the exercise Carl Miller told the children they *must* perform. Louise clutched her new cardigan around her shoulders—the sweater her mother implored her to substitute with a coat—and stubbornly refused. Eunice gave up, knowing that Louise at other times would not join in activities, remaining inside the Pleasant Hill School rather than frolicking with others during recess. *That's just Louise*, Eunice said to herself. Then she checked on her little brother, Leland. Eunice was worried about him because he, usually so energetic, was growing listless. She ordered him to keep exercising.

Outside, the white was turning gray. Evening was upon them. Maxine Brown thought of her parents preparing dinner in their warm underground home. *Do they miss us?* she wondered. *Do they know where we are?* She shivered and nudged closer to her sister Rosemary's shoulder.

✳✳✳✳✳

In her small kitchen, Geneva Miller desperately hoped her husband, Carl, and daughter, Mary Louise, had found a safe place to wait out the storm. Just in case he was trying to make it home, she lighted a candle and placed it in the window.

When the storm blew in that morning, she had been milking the cows in the barn. Louis was alone in the house so she ran back to check on him, leaving the cows half milked. Three times through-out the day she bundled up in her warmest clothing to return to the barn to finish the milking. Each time, she thought she heard a voice say, "You'd better not go." Geneva wondered if she were crazy to pay attention to a disembodied voice but knew that it probably was a good idea to stay with the baby now. So she remained in the house.

⁎⁎*

Night came shortly after 6:00. It brought dusk but no peace to the little lost school bus. None of the freezing occupants was hungry or thirsty anymore. They grew colder as the storm tore on, and weary—too weary to continue exercising. The older ones, their strength flagging, held smaller ones on their laps to share warmth. The younger children seemed to take turns crying. No sooner had Laura Huffaker finished a bout of panic than Maxine Brown began to whimper, then Mary Louise Miller. Blanche Stonebraker men-tioned to no one in particular that she could not feel her toes. Clara Smith, who had always hated the itchy wool stockings her grand-mother knitted for her, now felt grateful for their density. The wind continued to rock the lost vehicle. The gale's constant whine barely bothered the children anymore. They had become accustomed to the sound.

Eunice Frost knew that in the moonless dark, nobody would be able to find the bus—even if somebody were looking for them. Their parents probably assumed they were all safe and warm in a neighbor's house or in one of the schoolhouses, but nothing could be confirmed because only the Stonebrakers had a telephone. Prairie people always took care of each other. Ever since Eunice could remember, when a neighbor was in trouble or death struck, the farm community pulled together whatever food or help was available. The children had always been able to rely on the support of friends and neighbors. But hostile elements—seemingly greater than the combined force of protective grown-ups—were against them.

Leland Frost was growing heavy on his sister Eunice's lap. She looked down at his sleepy face and prodded him awake. "Do not sleep," she warned. He just looked confused. It was no use explaining to him the danger they were in. She talked to him and rubbed his feet and hands to keep the circulation going. At one point, she relaxed and almost dozed off, but then Miller called her name sharply: "Eunice!" She sat upright again and jostled Leland. He cried that he must go to the bathroom, so she directed him to the back of the bus, where he relieved himself into the drift that had poured through the broken windows. He had to squint against the blowing gale.

Clara Smith worried about her two younger brothers who rode on horseback to and from their own country school. Despite herself, she envisioned them freezing on a horse that was suffocating because of the fine snow. And what of her sister, Nora? The west-side bus had not reached the school by the time Miller's bus left; hopefully the western youngsters were safe.

The wind rippled the children's skirts and trousers and chilled their faces, so they found it warmer to huddle next to each other than to exercise. (Indeed, the bus was so small that huddling was inevitable.) Some stretched their legs out on the floor, overlapping each other's limbs. They could not quite get comfortable in the cramped bus, but Miller told them the discomfort would keep them awake. *Even the horses must be warmer in their stalls than we are in this wretched bus,* Alice thought as she gathered Laura closer to her. *At least the horses have hay.*

❄✳❄✳❄

The seven west-side children and driver Oscar Reinert were becoming restless at being cramped inside the Crum house. The fun of playing all day was turning to fitfulness. They could not leave the house for any reason, except to go to the privy, because they might get lost in the storm. Plains blizzards were known to be instantly disorienting so a common practice at the onset of winter was to string a "lifeline" rope linking the house, the barn, the well, and the outhouse. At the Crum place, when the youngsters had to relieve themselves, they formed a human chain against the outside walls of the house by holding hands. Erma Crum took the girls to one side of the house and the men took the boys to the other. That night, the children took turns sleeping crosswise on the big bed, listening to the fierce wind whistling around the corners of the house. They were grateful for the extra warmth of huddling next to each other under the blankets because the cold air that usually lingered near the walls was shoving its way into the middle of the room tonight. A mile away, there was no bed, no warmth, nothing hot to drink, and no human chain to form as the little bus on the prairie filled with snow and despair.

"Charley!" Carl Miller called out. "Kenneth! Mary Louise!" The wind never tired. Its shrieking muffled Miller's voice. Maxine Brown did not feel sleepy at all, and wasn't that odd? The recurring image of a steaming teakettle on a big hot iron stove kept her warm and comfortable. What an inviting thought. Soothing. Her big sister, Rosemary, shifted beneath her. Rosemary was not thinking of a steaming teakettle on a big hot iron stove. She was thinking that this was an eternal night.

Charley Huffaker looked about at his five siblings. He could not see them clearly in the dark, but knew by their drooping heads and their voices that everyone was growing tired. All but Alice were younger than he. Ten-year-old Max, wearing rubber boots, snuggled next to him. The children from his family appeared all right: drained and drowsy but still themselves. Their mother had always made certain her children dressed warmly, and looking around, Charley noticed that others were not so well clad. Louise Stonebraker had only that light sweater, and she was waning. Charley called out sharply: "Louise!" She looked around until her eyes focused on him. "Stay awake!" he told her. She nodded dazedly.

Mary Louise Miller, whom Charley did not know very well because she was new this year and in the younger class, only wore a jacket over her short dress. All the girls wore stockings beneath their dresses and all wore dresses; no pants. Fourteen-year-old Clara Smith, sitting opposite Charley, wore long stockings, new shoes, a dress, and a light coat. She was taking care of little Kenneth Johnson, who had no brothers or sisters. Bryan Untiedt was still wearing the coat Carl Miller loaned him when he and Clara went outside to search for a fence line, so Bryan should have been the warmest of all. Bryan called out names and cuffed his brothers Ome and Arlo, nine and eight respectively, so they would stay awake. Bobbie Brown, who hadn't had time to put on his coat that morning, looked wan. Charley Huffaker noticed that his cousins Eunice and Leland Frost were awake. Charley did not have to worry about his older sister, Alice. She was naturally a take-charge sort of person, and though he noticed her eyelids fluttering occasionally, she always snapped out of it and called out someone else's name. Laura sat on Alice's lap; Lena leaned against Alice.

The hour hand on Carl Miller's pocket watch moved slowly to midnight and then to 2:00 a.m. Throughout the long night, sleep taunted the children, but Miller and the older ones slapped, shoved, and shouted to keep it at bay. To sleep was to die. Miller periodically rallied them to exercise, and because these children obeyed their elders even against the seduction of sleep, they jumped, boxed, and jogged in place. In this dim, freezing bus, where the howling wind produced so much noise their ears were growing numb to it, they called out each other's names, sat on each other's laps, and tried to fight sleep. Crammed twenty-one in a tiny bus, they were each other's only warmth.

All night long.

Just before 6:00 a.m. the black outside turned gray and then white as the sun rose over Kansas, as it had for thousands of previous mornings. Despite the coming sunrise, no heat penetrated the opaque snow into the bus. The children all knew they were colder than even last night. They were later told that the temperature hung at twenty degrees below zero that morning, and the wind dashed snow across the unbroken plains at seventy miles an hour. The combined forces created a windchill of minus 105 degrees Fahrenheit.

Exercise! someone called out against the wailing wind. Some of the children—those who could—stood and moved their freezing extremities. Laura Huffaker reached up to tighten her hat strings but her fingers were too cold to move. She looked so frustrated that Alice murmured soothingly in her ear.

It was 7:00 a.m. and the back quarter of the bus was filled with snow. The children were half awake and exhausted. Somehow they had made it through the night. Was it morning? Had this horrible night ended? With soft morning light glowing through the frosted windows, Clara noticed icicles hanging from the ceiling and symmetrical little drifts of snow in each crack of the bus wall. It would be beautiful in any other situation, she thought. The children gazed at each other's matted hair and droopy, red eyes. Someone smirked and remarked about their silly appearances. The laughter felt good, and they let it bubble up in an effort to buoy their spirits. It was, after all, a new day, and the eternal night *had* ended. Maybe this imprisonment would end soon, too.

Maybe.

Carl Miller gazed around at the haggard children who were doing their best to pretend their situation was not as drastic as it was. He would not give up. It was time to start exercising again, he ordered. "Stand up! Move!" His daughter, Mary Louise, dragged herself to a standing position. Louise Stonebraker, who balked at exercising, sat listlessly in her birthday sweater against the snowbank at the back of the bus.

Miller contemplated his next action. Now that morning had arrived with no rescue and Louise Stonebraker had faded to the point of danger, he knew what must be done. He *must* go for help. He murmured to Clara his fear that if he were not to seek help, he could be prosecuted. He asked Bryan to return his coat, then announced, in a voice that conveyed more hope than he felt, that he would leave now, and when he returned with rescuers they would all eat a hearty pancake breakfast. "Keep exercising," he told them. He looked especially hard at the older children, emphasizing to them the importance of keeping up the exercising and the spirits of the younger children.[10] Clara knew the dreadful hopelessness out there because she had tried to fight through the vicious wind in search of a fence line the previous day. She felt that Miller would never return. Eunice Frost heard him add that the youngsters should pray: "Pray that I find help or that someone finds you here."

Eunice prayed. Silently, she pleaded with God to lead somebody to their school bus and to protect them from death. For a moment she felt peace, then the roaring wind filled her head again. She hoisted Leland upright.

Charley Huffaker wondered about Carl Miller's state of mind; he thought Miller seemed desperate and confused. Then again, Charley realized he probably felt he had no choice but to leave. Miller took one final look around at the mass of children, jumping up and down in what now seemed like slow motion, then plunged into the blizzard. The door slammed behind him and the whiteness enclosed him.

He was gone.

They all, individually, felt suddenly so alone without their adult, their driver, their guardian.

Eunice Frost glanced past the children, who, no longer giggling, were moving oh so slowly in the frozen aisle. Louise Stonebraker—she with the light sweater; she who would not exercise, not even in the recess yard—was still seated on the bench where she had been all night. Eunice gasped sharply, quickly. "Louise!" she shouted. Louise's eyes had stopped blinking, frozen into a straight stare. Someone shoved her—hard—but Louise only stared. Alice Huffaker leaned toward Blanche and told her that her older sister was dead.[11]

That was the last thing Blanche would remember of this day—a day when, one by one, the children of the Pleasant Hill school bus would begin freezing to death.

CHAPTER FOUR

Waiting

AS THE EXHAUSTED CHILDREN in the Pleasant Hill school bus were trying to comprehend that Louise Stonebraker had fallen into an eternal sleep, Geneva Miller pulled her bedroom curtain aside and peered out. The storm blew as relentlessly as it had all night. Obviously, Geneva had not slept well for worrying about her husband, Carl, her daughter, Mary Louise, and the other schoolchildren. She supposed they were safe in the Pleasant Hill school buildings or in one of the nearby homes, but until she knew for certain, it would be a long day.

A skim of ice covered the water in the kitchen bucket. It must be dreadfully cold outside, she thought. She stirred a small fire in the iron kitchen stove to make a pot of coffee for herself and oatmeal for little Louis, who was wondering where his father and big sister were.

Geneva Miller was not alone in her sleepless worry. Bud and Hazel Untiedt paced the floor all night, checking on the light in their own window. Bud Untiedt resolved to set out on horseback in search of the children. The horses would instinctively know their way through the opaque snow.

❄✳❄✳❄

The stunned children of Pleasant Hill left Louise Stonebraker at the back of the wooden bus. It was shortly after sunrise on Friday,

March 27, 1931, but little sun penetrated the whirling snow. The wind wailed and whiteness still curtained the windows. The Chevrolet bus was but a dot on the vast and desolate prairie, enshrouded in drifts and doom.

The bus had thunked into the barrow pit of the gravel road that connected Towner, fourteen miles to the north of the bus, and Holly, seventeen miles to the south. The narrow road was sparsely traveled and served mainly to link dryland agricultural spreads around Towner, Sheridan Lake, and Chivington, to the larger town of Holly, population 971, and then on to Lamar, the seat of Prowers County and, with a population of 4,223, the unofficial capital of southeastern Colorado. This lonely road from Holly to Towner also served as the conduit through which farmers such as the Huffakers and Browns could get their eggs and milk to Holly and Lamar to sell them at market price. And Lamar had certain services exclusive to this part of Colorado. There was, for instance, the Charles Maxwell Hospital, privately owned and operated by Mayor Charles Maxwell, where most ill or injured people in the vast southeastern part of the state went; unless they were so bad off they had to be taken to Pueblo, 122 miles west.

Even on nice days there was only an occasional tin can of a car, truck, or horse-drawn farm wagon coming along this road, and in a dreadful blizzard certainly none would happen by. It was now midday on Friday—the children had left their homes on Thursday morning—but they had lost track of time because Carl Miller had the only pocket watch, and he was gone. Long gone, it felt to them. Did anyone miss them? Was anyone wondering why they had not returned home? Had any parents gone to the school to look for them?

An engine! Maxine Brown thought she heard a vehicle! But her older sister, Rosemary, knew it was just Maxine's imagination. Rosemary recognized the improbability of a truck or car or wagon being out in this weather, unless it contained people searching for the bus. Yet at the same time, she longed so very desperately for a car or a horse to somehow pass them, see them, rescue them.

Mary Louise Miller knew that her pony, Prince, at home in his lean-to stable, missed her. She did not get to ride him the previous afternoon because she was trapped in this bus with her daddy. Now he was gone, but she had faith in him. If anyone could find help, it would be her daddy.

❋❋❋❋*

At the Crum place, the west-side children were hungry. They had eaten their lunches the day before and the pantry was empty. Besides that, fuel for the stove was running low; the fire barely kept the chill at bay. Oscar Reinert and Albert Crum bundled into their warmest clothes and walked the half mile east to the school-houses to get coal. There, they found Franz Freiday, the junior high teacher, still stranded. He was grateful to help them carry coal to the Crum house and get something to eat there.[12] Shortly afterward, two more fathers arrived with a bucket of homemade donuts and boiled eggs. The children devoured the food and paid no attention to the adults conversing quietly—and in worried tones—near the door.

Clara Smith, the oldest, stood up and urged the others in the bus to do the same. It was important to keep moving. Yes, it was crowded, with twenty young people in this eleven-by-five-foot space that grew smaller with every inch of invading snow, but they must jump around more. Not easy; they had been in this diabolical vehicle now for nearly twenty-four hours and lethargy was invading. It would be so much more comfortable to sit and maybe cry, but the younger boys agreed that everybody had to keep moving.

Bryan Untiedt—a gawky twelve-year-old and the tallest pupil on the bus—was not yet adjusted to his unwieldy limbs and accidentally elbowed out the glass in the door's window. Now a vicious crosswind blew through the bus from the missing back windows to the front. No matter, keep exercising. Mr. Miller had ordered as much before he disappeared into the white, and they had better do as he said, because when he returned with help they would all eat pancakes. He promised.

Pancakes. Oddly, the thought of food did not inspire hunger; the children were past the point of hunger. But the thought of being home in a warm kitchen, smelling steaming, fresh, wheat pancakes, and not being so, so cold—it was really familiarity, comfort, and warmth they hungered for. But for now they should exercise. So they jumped around yet again, cuffing each other, pretending to be boxers and runners. But boxers and runners move quickly, and no matter how hard the Pleasant Hill children tried, their limbs would not respond normally. The air felt thick, as if their heavy arms and legs could not cut through it. How long could this go on?

And why was Bobbie Brown mumbling? Come to think of it, his eyes had been staring strangely since Carl Miller left.

The aisle was already too narrow, and now it was slippery. Bryan Untiedt, nearly twice the height of the youngest children, allowed the others to jostle him to the front of the bus, where he fell into the driver's seat. When Carl Miller left for help, he took back his sheepskin coat, and the chill that had invaded everyone else hours earlier now struck Bryan. He looked about for his own, lighter coat, but it was trampled underfoot in the aisle, along with a random glove, someone's hat, and an ice-coated leather shoe with its stiff tongue hanging out.

Alice Huffaker tried to keep her feet out of the others' way, but it was so crowded that their feet just stumbled over hers. Even when she stood and tried to jump, her friends kept stepping on her feet! She had been wearing overshoes; here was one, but the other was somewhere else. And her gloves were so soaked and so encrusted with ice that she flung them onto the floor. It could not possibly get any colder. What use were these sodden articles of clothing anyway?

Bobbie Brown, resting on the bench, did not want to think about anything or feel this cold any longer. Sleep would feel so wonderful. To sleep, to sleep. "Stop rubbing me and slapping me and calling my name," he muttered. There was so much noise; he wanted the din of the storm to go away, go away; he wanted to sleep, and now he was beginning, finally, to grow warm and comfortable. Why wouldn't his big sister, Rosemary, leave him alone? She kept chanting, *we can't let him die, we can't let him die*, then he was being lifted and laid across laps and rubbed. He drifted away, and nobody carried him anywhere, just laid him on the rear section of bench next to Louise Stonebraker.

Maxine Brown, eight years old, assumed that her older brother would awaken. Rosemary did not know how to react, and believed that when they all got warm, Bobbie would wake up. Her mind felt as frozen as the ice clutching the bus. Rosemary wondered if her mother had let her dog, Fritz, into the house so he would be warm. He always stayed outside, but it was so cold. *How can it be so cold?*

The children were in shock. They knew only to continue exercising; it was almost an obsession. They could not think properly. Someone just died? Impossible. The nightmare would end and they would be warm under the bed quilt and would wake and have a normal day filled with slopping the hogs and Mr. Miller's safe bus and reading and dreaded arithmetic and laughter and "fox and geese." This entrapment on the bus could not be real, for if it were, classmates would be dead—and nobody in this horrible bus was dead. Death happens in stories, in the newspaper, on the radio—to *other* people. Exercise. They must keep exercising. They must slap each other to stay awake.

What was wrong with little Kenneth Johnson? He gazed blankly and murmured that his daddy was coming to get them. What was he staring at? Keep your feet moving, Kenneth! He was so small, only seven years old, and because he had no brothers or sisters, he was everyone's responsibility. Someone slapped him, but he barely reacted. His mouth dropped open and spittle dripped onto his chin. Was he falling asleep on his feet? "Kenneth!" someone cried, but before anyone could catch him, he crumpled to the floor, dead.[13] Clara Smith carried him to the back and set him next to Louise Stonebraker and Bobbie in the snowy corner that served as the makeshift latrine. And morgue.

Eunice Frost's mind was numb, but she was vaguely alert enough to realize that if nobody found them today, they would all be dead tomorrow. Three classmates had just died in front of her, and she absolutely knew that death would strike again if they remained in this bus much longer. She squeezed her eyes shut and prayed once more that no one else would die. What time was it? Friday afternoon? It felt as if they had been in this cramped icebox for days, but as far as she could remember, it was just that morning that Carl Miller had left.

Blanche Stonebraker's stocking garters somehow became tangled in the bench near the door. Nobody knew that she was trapped in a sitting position. Nobody knew much of anything anymore.

❄❆❅❆❄

From the time his children did not arrive home from school on Thursday evening, Bud Untiedt worried. Like other parents, he assumed the children were safe at the schoolhouse, but he did not know, and he was helpless against the storm. It was midday Friday and although the wind was abating only slightly, Untiedt could wait no longer. Four of his children, as well as a girl in his charge, had boarded a school bus the previous morning and disappeared. His wife, Hazel, prepared enough food for the hungry children, whom he hoped were in the schoolhouses. Untiedt hitched two horses to a wagon loaded with blankets and food, and rode the mile to the Pleasant Hill School. Neither he nor the horse (whose mouth and nose Bud protected from the frigid wind with a gunny sack) could see more than a few yards, but he pursued the road, following the fence line (the only navigable object), until he reached the twin schoolhouses. Large snowdrifts piled against the north side of the structures, but the wind had blown the south side clear. Untiedt climbed down and forced open the door of the larger building. Snow had seeped through the cracks in the outside walls, piling up in a slope toward the ceiling. No children or teachers rushed to greet him. It was empty and cold. The smaller school building, where Freiday had been until a few hours ago, was also empty. Where were the children? Maybe they were safe in a warm house. He dreaded the possibility that they were on that frigid bus.

At the same time, Ernie Johnson and Dave Stonebraker also set out for the school. Johnson had packed sandwiches, assuming that the children were marooned in the schoolhouses without food. When they too found the schoolhouses empty, they set out in a frenzy for surrounding farmhouses. Visibility was low, but intermittently the wind calmed enough to see for miles.

It was now late afternoon on Friday, March 27, 1931, but the children had lost their sense of time. They had been cold for so long. Every so often, they drew deep breaths and yelled "He-e-elp!" as loudly as possible, but no one heard or came.

Rosemary heard an engine; she was certain of it. She and Alice Huffaker peered through the window but saw only white. They must go outside to investigate. The snow did not seem to be blowing as much as earlier. Where was Mr. Miller, and why hadn't he brought help? She and Alice must go outside and search for a clue to their location.

One of the smaller children thought he heard a car passing, too. *Someone must be out there—call to the driver!* Maxine began sobbing. She wondered why these cars did not stop for them, why they passed by so callously. Everyone was abandoning them!

Rosemary Brown told Alice Huffaker that the two of them must go outside and search for those passing cars, a fence line, or a house. Someone thought the schoolhouses stood in the distance, but nobody else saw anything but white. Unless . . . Rosemary pushed open the door and Alice followed. The wind smacked their bare faces and blew ice into their eyes. They had no way of knowing that they were heading due south along the Holly–Towner road, or that it was afternoon.

Alice heard a sound like rock hitting against rock. The *clunk, clunk* matched her footsteps. She looked down. Her feet thudded against the stone-hard dirt road, yet she felt nothing. Her dress blew up and flapped against her legs, but the skin, covered only by thin cotton stockings, had no sensation.

Rosemary marched ahead of Alice, plodding into the whiteness. She could not feel her legs moving, yet she knew they were. There was no time or space, just swirling, freezing blankness. All they needed to find was a reference point so they could survive. They kept walking forward, numb feet thumping the ground. Alice tugged on Rosemary's sleeve, which was pulled over her bare hand, and shouted that they must return to the bus before it disappeared. They turned to face the white sheet behind them. *Just walk*, they told themselves. The bus will be there. It was earlier. *Just walk*. Alice stumbled, landed on the hard ground, got up, walked on.

There was the bus, hidden in the blowing snow and ice. Alice fell just as her foot was about to reach the running board. She almost stayed on the frozen earth. It would have been so easy to just lie down and rest—but she knew that she must fight against the wind. She tried to grip the running board, but her stiff hands refused to respond. Then, somehow, she pulled herself upright. When Alice reached to grab the handle, Rosemary saw that her fingernails had turned black. Rosemary grabbed the door handle and tugged with her, but the wind buffeted against them and held the door closed. They pounded to get the attention of their classmates, who thrust themselves against the door to force it open. Rosemary and Alice struggled aboard, pushing each other in, then the door slammed behind them. They told their classmates that they had found nothing, that there were no autos, no schoolhouses, no fence posts, nothing.

❄❅❆❅❄

Others fought against the wind that afternoon. On the same road as the stalled bus, Elbern Coons and his eighteen-year-old son, Elbern Jr., left their stalled car and now on foot felt their way along a barbed-wire fence. They had been in Lamar, forty-nine miles to the southwest, but at the storm's first warning had set out in their auto for their home near Pleasant Hill. Unbeknownst to them, a stranded school bus full of frightened and dead children stood less than a quarter mile from their stalled 1928 Chrysler Imperial four-door sedan. If Rosemary and Alice had continued walking south another hundred yards, they would have encountered the Coonses' car.

But what was this that the Coonses discerned through the white? This fence ended at a building—a house! They pounded on the door. Andy Reinert opened it and urged them into the warmth.

❄❄✳❄

Arlo Untiedt was drifting off to sleep. The older children took turns rubbing and smacking him. Mary Louise Miller, whose father had walked into the white abyss hours ago and disappeared (where could he be?), was quiet and unfocused. They pleaded with her to move around. Nobody dared glance at the snow-choked back of the bus where Louise Stonebraker sat, stiff and glassy-eyed, her hair frozen in thick, dark strands, and where Kenneth Johnson hunched, stony. Blowing flakes settled on both. Bobbie Brown looked oddly peaceful, as if he would wake refreshed. He was dead, but the children on the bus did not have the emotional energy to comprehend that fact. They were exhausted and frightened; many hovered on the edge of delirium.

Bryan Untiedt and Charley Huffaker decided that they, too, must search for landmarks. Alice and Rosemary had tried, and the previous day Bryan and Clara had tried, and each time no one was able to see beyond an outstretched arm. As the oldest boys, Bryan and Charley felt obligated to try again. As Alice and Rosemary had done only minutes earlier, they pushed the door open and squinted against the snow that hit their faces like flying sand. They groped along the wooden bus from the door to the headlights, but the wind nearly knocked them over. Charley feared that if they left the vehicle they would lose their bearings, so they reboarded the bus. Clara lent Bryan her coat but was grateful when he gave it back a few minutes later. Everyone crowded together, even more than the tiny space necessitated, and the shared warmth helped—a little.

*****

The wind was finally subsiding at the Crum household. Oscar Reinert went outside to see if his car engine would fire up, and when it did, he went back inside to inform the children they would all be going home. They piled happily into his car, and he set out in the crisp 4:00 p.m. air to deliver them to their families.

*****

Bryan knelt to rub his brother Arlo's hands and legs, then commented to Clara that Arlo's eyes were growing glassy. Clara noticed the eeriness of Bryan's own eyes. No one exercised anymore; the children of the Pleasant Hill School were giving up hope. They were lost to the world in this blizzard on the endless Colorado plains, their protector had disappeared, and as far as they knew, nobody searched for them. They did not know visibility was improving outside, that the storm was finally subsiding.

Bryan, hunched over the steering wheel, muttered, "Oh, this is hell." No one argued. Nobody had the energy or the will. Nobody seemed to remember Miller's admonition to keep moving no matter what. The day crept on, but no one knew it was nearly 5:00 p.m. on Friday, March 27. Nobody did the arithmetic to figure out that they had been in the death bus for nearly thirty-three hours.

In the bus, a listless child remarked that it was growing warmer. Warmer? How can it be warmer inside when it is colder outside? Others agreed, *it really is warmer*, and they began shedding their hats and coats. They concluded that they must form a pile on the floor. The bigger children would lie on top of the smaller. Yes, that was what they would do!

Sleep called—it had been an exhausting day and night. What harm could it do? The smaller ones took off their coats and blanketed the icy floor with them. The older ones took off their coats to spread on top of the pile. How wonderful that it was no longer cold. The little ones lay down on the floor, atop the soft coats. It was so warm as sleep beckoned to this pile of humanity on the slick floor of the wooden school bus.

Horse harnesses rattling, Charley Huffaker thought through the haze of his oncoming dreams. *Perhaps not*. But then someone else heard it, too, and the noise grew louder, and then the unmistakable *clip-clop* of horse hooves on the frozen ground—and it must be true because everyone heard it, right? The problem was, it disturbed their warm sleep . . . *clip-clop, clip-clop, clip-clop* . . .

A gust blasted through the Pleasant Hill bus as Bud Untiedt wrenched open the door and struggled to comprehend the horror that confronted him.

CHAPTER FIVE

Blankets
and Fried Potatoes

BUD UNTIEDT HAD NEVER heard such wailing and sobbing and rejoicing. Inside the bus was death—and life; little people glassy eyed and babbling. Dave Stonebraker, standing directly behind Bud, uttered, "Oh my God," when he saw his frozen daughter, Louise, half covered with snow.[14] He carried Mary Louise Miller, huddled near the door, quickly to the wagon. Untiedt picked up his fading son, Arlo, and took him to the wagon. He returned for his eldest son, Bryan, who was sitting in the driver's seat half delirious, but Bryan waved him away and told him to take the others first. Untiedt followed his son's direction, then returned to urge him into the wagon. Charley Huffaker, able to walk independently, was one of the first to climb into the wagon. The two fathers carried the remaining children, some of whom were hysterical with grief and joy, and unable to walk on their numb feet. Clara Smith was one of the last to climb up. She felt bad that the smaller children were beneath her, but there was no room to readjust and put them on the bigger children's laps. The fathers threw blankets, already damp from the snow, over the chilled pile of humanity and urged the horses forward. The dead were left on the bus bench.

The wind calmed enough that Untiedt and Stonebraker could see to drive the horses. Stonebraker's house lay a mile across the snowy fields, but Andy and Fern Reinert's ranch home was only a half mile away along the road.[15] It was just after 5:00 p.m.

In her small kitchen, the pregnant Fern Reinert stirred the potatoes and macaroni bubbling on the stove. She was thankful there was enough food in the house to feed the two unexpected visitors—Elbern Coons and his eighteen-year-old son, Elbern Jr.—as well as her husband, Andy, their two youngsters, and Andy's brother, Edwin, who lived nearby. The corncob and cow chip fuel supply would keep the four-room concrete-block house warm, even at these freezing temperatures.[16] Andy and Edwin sat at the kitchen table with the Coonses discussing the storm outside as the worst anybody could remember hitting this area. The toddlers, Lois and Earl, played quietly in the corner. A frantic knock at the door startled them.

Andy opened the door, and the chill blew in. Dave Stonebraker and Bud Untiedt gasped out the unbelievable news: They had just found a missing busload of children from the Pleasant Hill School; some were dead and some were alive but frostbitten, and many were incoherent. It was imperative to get these children into the warmth. The Coonses, though exhausted from a long day of fighting the storm, were instantly bundling into their outer wraps. They opened the door and all four men dashed to the wagon. Fern pulled blankets and extra clothing from the chest of drawers in the bedroom. She wondered how many children there were.

Fern Reinert knew that the Pleasant Hill School was where her younger brother and sister, Eunice and Leland Frost, and her cousins, the Huffaker children, attended classes. It was also the district for which Andy served on the school board. Maude Moser, who had lived with Andy's parents when Fern and Andy were newlyweds, taught there.

The door opened again, and Fern saw a young boy, eyes barely focusing, lying limp in Bud Untiedt's arms. Distress furrowed Untiedt's narrow face. He laid his son Arlo on the floor and began massaging his hands and face, trying to circulate the blood and reawaken the tissue.

The men carried child after child in from the wagon until the twenty-four-by-twenty-four-foot kitchen was filled with seventeen children, some crying. The fine slivers of ice that coated their hair and clothing melted onto the plank floor. Some knew where they were, others were confused. The less injured among them walked about until the elder Elbern Coons urged them to rest their frozen legs. They sat down, and a blanket was spread over them. Clara Smith looked down at her swollen legs and thought crazily, *This is how I would look if I were fat.*

Dave Stonebraker, in shock over his daughter Louise's death, dispatched Edwin Reinert, Andy's brother, to the Stonebraker residence because it had one of the few telephones in the district. His instructions were to call Holly; call Towner; call Tribune, Kansas; call everywhere until he reached a doctor. Also, he said to alert the parents that their children had been found and that most were alive, and to pass the word to all neighbors so they could help revive the children.

When Fern Reinert saw her younger siblings, Eunice and Leland Frost, she rushed to hug them and rub their hands and feet. Poor little Leland, she thought, he's only seven years old. She began to take off his shoes so she could massage some blood back into his feet, but Andy stopped her. He pointed out that Leland's shoes were frozen to his feet, and that they dare not try to remove them until the skin began to thaw. Fern's throat felt tight, and she quickly stood and returned to the stove so Leland would not see her cry. Noticing his wife on the brink of tears, Andy thought that to spare Fern and their own two children the horror and impending chaos of the long night, it would be better to remove all three to her parents' house. There, she could inform the Frosts that their two youngest children, Eunice and Leland, were at her house, frostbitten but alive. Fern hugged her sister Eunice and stared at her in horror, but Eunice did not entirely comprehend it. Through the haze of motion around and above her, Eunice knew she was at her sister's house. She knew time was passing at a different pace for the fast-moving, worried adults than for her. She had not realized in the bus that her feet were slowly freezing, but now, as her extremities began to warm up, she felt a painful tingling in her feet. Sometimes she was aware of classmates sitting next to her, and the warm air from the stove radiating toward her, but sometimes her mind did not register these swirling impressions at all. The men sat the children upright along the kitchen walls, warning them not to fall asleep. They undressed some of the children and swathed them in the Reinerts' clothing. Dry blankets were laid over them. As their body temperatures rose, some children began shivering for the first time that day. Others could move their limbs only laboriously and painfully. Mary Louise Miller and Arlo Untiedt barely moved. Bud Untiedt helped Stonebraker, Reinert, and the Coons men massage the children's hands and feet with snow and salt—the common remedy for frostbite.[17] Untiedt's ten-year-old daughter, Evelyn, collapsed while standing in front of the cookstove and holding onto the railing. Untiedt caught her as she fell, then asked her to help him rub her brother Arlo. His request for help was a ruse to keep Evelyn alive, but Untiedt did not share this with his daughter that night. He knew it was important for her to focus on something while her body stabilized.

Alice Huffaker felt someone cutting the too-tight elastic that secured her stockings to her swollen thighs. Alice looked at the purplish-red skin as the stockings were pulled off. Her legs had no sensation. But now grains of snow bit her, then salt, as the men dipped her hands and feet into pans of snow and ice, then rubbed them down with salt.

Fern checked the potatoes. They were about halfway finished frying. The aroma awakened the children's senses, and all of a sudden, those who could balance on their stiff legs crowded around the stove grabbing at the hot potato sticks. Charley Huffaker—whose feet moved normally and who, incredibly, had not even a tinge of frostbite—planted himself by the stove and ate until his stomach was filled. Even Eunice Frost in her half-conscious state devoured potatoes. The adults debated whether to let the weakened children eat half-cooked potatoes, but it had been thirty-three hours since their last meal. Andy hid the pot of macaroni because eating too much too soon might upset their stomachs. He knew a doctor must tend to them as soon as possible. Some children were near death; many others would be fortunate to walk again.

Mary Louise Miller barely responded when Andy Reinert prodded her and spoke to her. Her heartbeat was weak. Dave Stonebraker knelt by his daughter Blanche and eased swollen feet out of her leather shoes. Dipping into a pan of snow, he rubbed the icy crystals on her feet and legs up to the knees. Her arms and hands were also stiff; the surface layers of skin frozen to above the elbow. Blanche saw her father through heavy-lidded eyes. The fog now cleared that had covered her brain since her sister Louise died, and Blanche began to sob. Her father spoke softly to her and continued rubbing her frozen limbs. He told her that someone had gone to their house to call a doctor and that they all had to stay where they were until medical help arrived.

Blanche looked down at Andy Reinert's shirt, which someone had put on her. It covered her from collarbone to ankle. When her father asked if she wanted anything from home, Blanche responded, "Can you have Mama send my pajamas?" Her father grinned and told her to be strong and that soon she would be at home wearing her own pajamas. He hoped his promise would become truth. Blanche was one of the worst off. Her fingers were swollen and stiff; she could not move them on her own. The surface flesh on her calves and lower arms was frozen hard. He knew her mind was not working properly because she repeated questions. Her mouth could barely open, so her words were slurred. He realized the likely possibility of her death: two Stonebraker girls dead in one day. Dave Stonebraker took a deep breath and forced himself to put aside the realization of Louise's death, because his great responsibility now was to save his youngest and to help other fathers save their children. There was no time for grief.

Fern Reinert packed changes of clothing for herself and her children, and one of the men drove them in a horse-drawn wagon to her parents' home about a mile east. The snow had stopped and the wind was calm enough to travel that short distance without difficulty. Before leaving, Fern kissed her siblings Eunice and Leland and told them that soon, they too would be going home. She hoped it was true.

Word spread. John Kenneth Herrick, a farmhand at the Frost residence, heard about the busload of children from Fern Reinert when she arrived around 5:45 p.m., and he set out on foot to see how he could help. Claude Frost followed him soon after. Edwin Reinert, who had gone for a telephone, alerted other neighbors. Every time the door opened, more neighbor men arrived to help massage frozen limbs and keep children awake. A pot of soup was set on the stove. A neighbor brought diesel fuel to massage into frostbitten skin, hoping to draw the cold out slowly. Someone opened a bottle of moonshine hoping to warm the children from the inside out, and one by one, mouths were opened and a tablespoonful of whisky poured into each.[18]

It burned all the way down Eunice's throat. Now fully awake, she looked around for her little brother, Leland, who had kept her lap warm the past day and a half on the bus. He was in the corner with their father, Claude, who was rubbing salt on Leland's legs. She did not even remember seeing him walk in! Eunice realized that someone was rubbing snow and salt on her legs as well. They were purple and blisters were beginning to form on the warming skin.

They felt so heavy, and Eunice could scarcely feel the hands working the abrasives into her skin. She lifted her hands, but it felt as if they were encased in lead mittens. Someone handed her crackers and a bowl of soup and helped her lift the spoon to her mouth. At least her tongue had not lost any sensation—that food tasted delicious.

Alice Huffaker noticed that she was lying on a blanket on the floor of someone's kitchen and that many adults were milling about, rubbing salt and snow on everyone's legs. And then she remembered: She and her friends had been far too long in the Pleasant Hill school bus. Now they were all in—(What was the name of the family that owned this house? Was it her cousin Fern's?)—well, they were in a damp, noisy house. Her legs burned. She looked down and noticed blisters popping out on the surface of her strangely puffed-out legs. Salt, she remembered. Someone had rubbed snow, then salt on her legs.

Clara Smith's feet had swollen so much that her new shoes were coming apart at the seams. She unlaced the shoes and eased them off—her hands functioned well enough, with only a little numbness in the fingertips—and massaged her feet. The skin still felt cold, even though she was sitting near the stove. The oddest thing was looking at these swollen, purple, sensationless lumps and knowing that they were her feet. Clara wondered how Arlo Untiedt was doing. He had been at the bottom of the pile, she remembered suddenly, and he was small. Had he been crushed by the others?

Arlo lay motionless on a blanket near the stove. Bud Untiedt frantically slapped his youngest son's pallid cheeks. Bryan, lucid after his snack of crisp, starchy potatoes, knelt by his father and brother. Bryan apologized to his father for hitting his brothers Arlo and Ome while they were on the bus, explaining that he was only trying to help them stay awake.

❄✳❄✳❄

In Tribune, Kansas, thirty-two miles northeast of the Pleasant Hill School, telephone operator Pearl Bennett picked up the ringing long-distance line. It was close to 7:30 p.m., March 27, and she had been dutifully manning the town switchboard all day, hoping the storm was finally subsiding. The voice from Towner on the crackling wire relayed the frantic call just received from a farmhouse fourteen miles south of there: A bus full of children, some near death and others whose hands and feet were frozen, needed a doctor as soon as possible. Was there anyone in Tribune who could make it across the snowdrift-covered roads to the Andy Reinert ranch and treat these children?

Bennett summoned the town physician, Dr. Lemly Hubener, who warned her that the roads might prove impassable, but that he would gather his medical kit and enlist townspeople with autos to form a caravan to try to reach the Reinert place in Colorado. Bennett called every man in and near town who had a phone, then stayed by her switchboard awaiting further instruction.

Dr. F. E. Casburn received a similar call at his home in Holly and made the same decision as his colleague in Kansas. He gathered six men: Mayor W. A. Kirby, Vaughn Swafford, Millard Brown, Fred Woods, Jim Miller, and Don Reish. Kirby's heavy Lincoln led the four-car caravan. The men chained their cars together, bumper to bumper, to ram through snowdrifts.

In Lamar, forty-nine miles southwest of the Reinert ranch, reporters at the *Lamar Daily News* searched for information about a missing school bus. Reports had arrived that a rural district school bus had departed from the Pleasant Hill School, between Holly and Towner, on Thursday morning to deliver the children home before the storm hit, and that none of the children had been seen since. United Press Association wire-service member newspapers in cities as distant as New York and as near as Denver requested photographs, updates, and speculation about the missing bus. Lamar reporters could not yet help. They did not know where the bus was, but they planned to dispatch reporters and photographers to the scene as soon as it was found.

The Pleasant Hill death bus was about to become a national story.

Charles Maxwell, Lamar mayor and owner of the city's private hospital, pondered the news he had just heard. These children, the ones lucky enough to be alive, would need the best medical care that southeastern Colorado could provide. That meant his facility and his benevolence, and as one of the city's leading citizens and benefactors, he was equal to the challenge. This was Maxwell's second term as Lamar's mayor; he had also served as town clerk. He had moved to Colorado in 1881 and now owned businesses including a bank, a mill, and a hotel in Lamar. Since 1921 he had significantly funded the First Church of the Nazarene, and continued to do so throughout the Depression years. The hospital he built had fifty beds, a capacity far surpassing other similarly sized Colorado towns. Maxwell often paid the hospital bills for patients who had no money. And conveniently, one of his physicians, Dr. Napoleon M. Burnett, had recently completed a course in frostbite care.

The Maxwell Hospital was obviously the place for the children; nonetheless, driving across the roads that were alternately swept clean and blocked by ten-foot-high snowdrifts promised to be difficult, if not impossible. Maxwell telephoned a local amateur aviator named Jack Hart, who nervously agreed to carry out the important mission of transporting nurses to the Reinert place by air and bringing the endangered children to Lamar. As soon as the sun shone on Saturday and the wind stayed down, Hart told Maxwell, he would be able to fly.

❄❄❄❄❄

By 9:00 p.m. Maxine Brown was beginning to warm up. She suddenly realized how dreadfully fatigued she was. She tried to sleep, but adults kept shaking her awake and rubbing her hands, reminding her that if she fell asleep she would die. She was too tired to care, but finally kept her eyes open and let her brain sink into a slumber. This packed room—as crowded in its own way as the bus, but not cold—exhausted her further with so many men moving around, stepping over the children, talking to them, tucking the blankets more securely around their shoulders, rubbing their feet, and helping them sip hot water. And where was her big sister, Rosemary? She had seen her brother Bobbie go to sleep. *Where was he now?* she wondered. *He could not possibly be dead, as others seemed to believe. But was he?*

By 11:00 p.m. the men rubbing snow and distillate on the frostbitten children resolved that Mary Louise Miller and Arlo Untiedt were dead. The men had been massaging them both for hours near the warm stove without any signs of life, and they knew they had to acknowledge the reality.[19] The rescuers did not want to upset the surviving children, however, so they kept it quiet. Dave Stonebraker found the situation difficult, especially because Mary Louise Miller was a close friend of Blanche's. The Stonebrakers would always stop by the Miller farm on Sundays to pick up Mary Louise for Sunday School.

The gigantic spring blizzard that claimed the lives of Louise Stonebraker, Bobbie Brown, Kenneth Johnson, Arlo Untiedt, and Mary Louise Miller (and perhaps Carl Miller as well—he had not been seen since setting out for help early that morning) had not singled out southeastern Colorado, this school bus, or these five young people. The unprecedented cold and snow had struck all of Colorado.

In Denver, Frederick G. Bonfils, owner of *The Denver Post*, received early news of the bus tragedy.[20] Bonfils ran one of the most notorious and successful scandal sheets in the United States—a reputation of which he was quite proud. His was a rag with blaring red-colored sensational headlines ("Does It Hurt to Be Born?") and sleazy business practices. The masthead of the paper bragged that the *Post* was "The Best Newspaper in the U.S.A.," yet he was far more interested in what was happening in Colorado than what was happening anyplace else in the world. "A dogfight on Sixteenth Street [in Denver] is a better story than a war in Timbuktu," he once pronounced. Many Denver businessmen advertised in his newspaper rather than in the rival *Rocky Mountain News* because of Bonfils's threat to exclude their wives from membership in social clubs or to vilify their businesses in print. Fred Bonfils's genius hinged on the unscrupulous; he pretty much ran Denver.

The promotions-minded Bonfils instantly recognized that his readers would thrive on forlorn little country children in faraway rural Colorado being trapped in a marooned wooden school bus during the worst blizzard in fifty-six years—and the heroic efforts being mounted to save them. Bonfils believed that if he could publish a story about someone worse off than his Depression-weary readers, they would eagerly hand three cents to the corner newsboy for the latest edition, then hunger for more details the next day, and the day after that. And the more sensationally the package was presented, the longer he could capitalize on the tragedy. Profit, prestige, and power motivated Bonfils, and now he scrambled to organize a plan for wringing every conceivable emotion out of this event for as long as he could keep it alive.

To make the most of what he would trumpet as "The Towner School Bus Tragedy" (although the village of Towner had nothing to do with the unfolding story), he would first need an airplane.

❉❉❉❉❉

The air in the Reinert house grew fetid. The stench emitting from the children who had soiled their clothing soaked into the mattresses and blankets and into the Reinerts' clean, dry clothes. Many perspiring men worked in this small space where fresh air was scarce, and it was too cold outside to open the door for ventilation. Snow and ice melted from clothes and shoes, soaking the wood floor; heat from the stove could not evaporate the moisture fast enough. The salty, warm scent given off earlier by the partially fried potatoes had long since been overwhelmed.

Around midnight of Friday, March 27, seven men from Holly arrived at the Reinert ranch. In their exhaustion and numbness, the children did not recognize that the adults ministering to them were now new faces and that one was a physician. Reinert, Untiedt, Stonebraker, Johnson, Frost, both Coons men, and the others who had been working on the children for five and a half hours trying to draw out the frostbite, knew the reinforcements could help. It was now entirely clear that Mary Louise Miller and Arlo Untiedt were dead, bringing the number of casualties to five. Dr. Casburn and the other Holly men took over for the weary fathers and neighbors. By now, the outer layers of frostbitten skin were thawing, shooting pain through the awakening nerves. Blanche Stonebraker felt that a hundred needles were tapping on her hands and feet; those needles would plague her constantly for the next three months.

With the dying of the storm came the decision to retrieve the three bodies from the bus. The men stopped their car just short of the dark vehicle. Shards of glass spiked the running board under the window that Bryan Untiedt had accidentally knocked out. The men stepped up and through the bus door, which was hanging open. The inside of the bus was no warmer than the wide prairie. Louise Stonebraker was half buried in the snowbank on the death bench, and nearby were Kenneth Johnson and Bobbie Brown. Their faces were as pallid as the snow piled around them. No sound disrupted the eerie stillness. One of the men stepped forward toward Kenneth. He picked up the seven-year-old boy, who remained in a stiff sitting position, and carried him out of the bus as he would a baby. The others picked up the remaining frozen bodies, set them in the car, and headed for the Brown household. There, the men helped Elmer Brown rub their cold limbs, hoping to revive them, but knowing they could not.[21]

Dr. Lemly Hubener arrived from Tribune with his three-car, twenty-three-man escort a short time before dawn on Saturday, March 28.[22] Some sections of the road were blown clean of snow, whereas other places were completely blocked. Plunging through the drifts took precious time. Neither physician had many other ideas for emergency first aid than the neighbors had already used, but they urged the quick removal of survivors to a hospital, where the room temperature could be regulated and pneumonia and gangrene

The Pleasant Hill school bus tragedy fast became international news. This is a picture postcard commemorating the event; notice the wording beneath the image. The cloudiness in the rear windows is an interior snowbank resulting from snow blowing through broken windows. The snowbank became a morgue, where survivors placed their deceased classmates. Carl Miller opened the hood in an unsuccessful attempt to start the engine.

forestalled. The nearest facility was Charles Maxwell's hospital in Lamar, forty-nine miles distant. Maybe soon it would be warm enough to melt the snow from the roads. In any case, the children could not be moved until daylight.

❋❋❋❋❋

A candle still burned in the window of Carl and Geneva Miller's farmhouse. Through her fitful sleep, Geneva heard noises outside the front door. At last, Carl and Mary Louise were home! She grabbed the lantern and rushed to the door. Instead of her husband and daughter, three somber neighbors stood silent and then apologized for waking her, adding that they hoped she was well. She invited them into her tiny, neat kitchen. One of the men informed her that the bus had been found and the children were at Andy Reinert's home. He cleared his throat nervously. Before he could speak, Geneva asked quietly, knowingly, "Are any of them dead?" One responded that doctors were at the farmhouse working to help the children. Geneva pressed for an answer. "Everything possible is being done," one man replied. He explained that because his group had left the farmhouse while neighbors were still trying to revive Mary Louise, they did not know for certain whether she was dead or alive. The men also informed her that Carl had left the bus early that morning, and they assumed he must have found shelter. Geneva was not convinced, for she knew that if her husband were alive and able, he would have returned to help the children.

Nonetheless, she built a fire in the stove, made a pot of coffee, and agreed to the suggestion that she visit with Carl's nearby parents for a day or two. The four sat solemnly around the small table, and when day broke, Geneva woke her small son, Louis, gathered a few items of clothing, and rode off in their wagon to the home of her in-laws. Her arrival brought to them the news of the Pleasant Hill school bus. Together they worried about Carl and Mary Louise.

CHAPTER SIX

"Ship of Mercy"

THE COMMOTION AT the Reinert ranch lessened a bit on Saturday, March 28. Weary neighbors returned home in their cars and wagons once the sun rose. The wind had dropped, the blizzard was gone, and the sun shone bright—typical in Colorado after a spate of bad weather. It was a beautiful day but for the death hovering over Pleasant Hill.

The neighbor men had their own chores waiting at home—frozen cattle carcasses to remove, leaking shed roofs to fix, and frightened children to soothe. Despite their exhaustion and pity for the families of the deceased and injured children, they felt grateful for the health and safety of their own families. Farm life on the Colorado plains dealt unwelcome surprises throughout the year, and they were reluctantly accustomed to them—but nothing like this. Those who prayed did so; others simply hugged their children and wives more earnestly than usual before falling into bed.

John Kenneth Herrick returned to the Claude Frost farm to carry out his daily duties as ranch hand. As he walked the half-mile home, he relived in his mind the fatiguing night spent rubbing frostbitten limbs and peering into drooping eyes.

Conversations the previous night touched upon many unanswered questions: Had the teachers made it home safely? In which home had driver Carl Miller found refuge while rescuers were busy tending to his charges? Miller was a newcomer to the community and no one knew him well enough to guess his motivations, but some believed that the children were his first priority, and as such, the fact that he had not surfaced was surely an indication of his death. Herrick knew that a search party was being organized for Miller's body, but he was too weary to take part. He would care for the Frost farm animals and then settle in for a long nap.

The *Post*'s front page the day after the rescue. Though the newspaper maintained the story as headline news for almost a month, circulation did not increase. The "woman instructor missing" headline was erroneous.

At the Reinert ranch, Reuben Huffaker looked over his brood of six. Fourteen-year-old Alice, one of the most affected of the children, managed a faint grin for him. He hoped she would not lose any fingers or toes, but at this point the outlook was dubious. She seemed confused and unaware of her surroundings. Seven-year-old Laura and ten-year-old Max suffered no physical problems. The doctors had declared them, amazingly, frostbite free. Their worst problem was fatigue—easily remedied by a night of solid sleep—because none of the children had been allowed to sleep since Wednesday night. Reuben Huffaker was happy to tell Laura and Max that they would return home later in the day. The others would be going to the Maxwell Hospital or to doctors' homes in Holly. Charley Huffaker's extremities suffered no frostbite, but the physicians thought it prudent to send him to the Maxwell Hospital in case he developed pneumonia, which had afflicted him earlier in life. Carl and Lena were also relatively unharmed, but Reuben Huffaker agreed with the on-site doctors that they should be examined.

Walter Smith, Clara's older brother, was stranded in Hartman, west of Holly, during the blizzard. When he heard about the children's rescue, he hurried to the Reinert farm in search of his sister. Clara was overjoyed to see him and immediately asked about her younger brothers, Ralph and Louis. Walter had not stopped at his family's rented farm north of Hartman, so he did not know if they were safe, but he promised to find out. He carried the news to his parents that Clara was alive.

When Elmer and Margaret Brown arrived at the Reinert house, Margaret saw Maxine, her youngest child, sitting at the opposite side of the room. The crowd of neighbor men dwarfed Maxine's tiny frame. Margaret made her way through the throng and embraced her eight-year-old. "I could see every beat of your heart clear across the room," she told Maxine. It made no sense to Margaret that Maxine—who had been a three-pound baby—would survive, and Bobbie would be the one to die. Bobbie, though robust and active, had always disliked being wet and cold. He must have simply given in to the warm temptation of sleep. Margaret Brown wept. Why did this have to happen to her children? Her oldest daughter, Rosemary, stoic even at thirteen, had shown neither fear nor pain until her mother arrived. Then Rosemary—she who had been so strong for the younger children and so in charge of herself—saw her mama and like a child asked, "Did Bobbie wake up?" Margaret looked away in a vain attempt to hide her tears and replied, "No."

❄✳∗✳❄

Pilot Jack Hart, as commissioned by Charles Maxwell, set off from Lamar at about 10:00 a.m. on Saturday, March 28, 1931, with nurses Frances Delk and Julia Rybak. Twenty-two minutes later he located a field windswept clear of snow, and landed near the Reinert house.

Adults on the ground selected the two most seriously afflicted youngsters, Alice Huffaker and Blanche Stonebraker, to go on the first flight to the hospital. Neither Alice nor Blanche was lucid enough to care what was happening, though in better condition they would have appreciated the excitement of being in an *airplane*. All they knew was that strong men wrapped them in blankets, lifted them up into the plane—where it was noisy and the floor shook— and then different men lifted them down, carried them into a big building, and put them in bed.

Nurse Rybak made the trip with them; Nurse Delk stayed behind to tend to the children at the farmhouse. The successful journey instilled confidence in Hart, and he took off for another trip to the Reinert farm, this time bringing along the hospital superintendent, Marie Wadham.

A survivor at the Reinert farm being transferred between Jack Hart's open-cockpit plane (left) and an ambulance-hearse (at right in the photo). Note the absence of snow from the windswept field.

Shortly after noon, another engine noise grew loud in the sky. A larger airplane, a Fokker named *The Fawn*, belonging to the wealthy Albert E. Humphreys, Jr., son of Denver's noted oil baron, Albert Humphreys, crossed the horizon and approached the bleak landscape. It had been sent courtesy of Fred Bonfils. Captain Eddie Brooks, whom Bonfils touted highly in his paper the following day, piloted what the *Post* would dub "the Ship of Mercy." Aboard were reporter Fred Warren, photographer Edward O. Eisenhand, and mechanics W. Babbitt and R. Weichel.

The rescue ship from Denver landed, its door opened, and Brooks and his passengers descended; all to the considerable amazement of the farm people, who generally would have expected such scenes from only a newspaper or motion picture newsreel. *The Fawn's* mission was to transport the remainder of children requiring prompt medical attention to the hospital in Lamar and, not incidentally, for Fred Bonfils and his newspaper to gather information for a front-page story. The least afflicted children would be driven to Lamar later that afternoon because the roads were clear enough for autos to make it, albeit with difficulty.

Reporter Warren and photographer Eisenhand got busy. Laura Huffaker, Evelyn Untiedt, Ome Untiedt, and Max Huffaker sat on the floor, leaning against a kitchen cupboard. A patchwork quilt that Dave Stonebraker had brought from home lay across their knees. Eisenhand snapped a photograph of the four stunned children; it would be published not only in the *Post* but in papers around the nation.

Warren spoke with some of the parents and neighbors. His observations and conversations would appear in print as an engrossing and powerful human interest story, one that would capture the attention of *Post* readers but not dishearten them with its overt tragedy. Turning to Bud Untiedt, the father of the oldest boy, Bryan Untiedt, Warren remarked: "What this story really needs is a hero. How would your son like to be the hero?" Clara Smith and Dave Stonebraker overheard the question but did not understand its significance until later, when the reporter's version of the tragedy was published.[23]

Pilot Brooks asked nurse Frances Delk how to proceed, and she recommended that the plane take Bryan Untiedt, Charley Huffaker, and Rosemary Brown to Lamar. Adults gathered up those children and carried them to the plane; Bud Untiedt and Nurse Delk accompanied them on the short flight to the hospital. The mechanics and the two *Post* men stayed behind.

Bryan, Charley, and Rosemary had been loaded so hastily onto the plane that photographer Eisenhand missed the picture of them being put aboard. He therefore asked if any local farm children would be willing to pose as Bryan in order to re-create the scene for *Post* readers. Herbert Speer, who was about Bryan's age, was wrapped in a blanket for the shot. The phony picture was printed the following day in the Sunday *Post* with Bryan's name beneath it.

The *Lamar Daily News* also showed up at the Reinert place. Publisher, editor, and writer Fred M. Betz, manager A. Boon McCallum, and photographers E. H. Applegate, Jr. and J. H. Ward traveled to the Pleasant Hill district to shoot photos of the schoolhouses, the stalled bus still sitting in the ditch, and the children being loaded into Jack Hart's airplane. Those photographs were displayed in the windows of the *Daily News* office, and some were reprinted in newspapers nationwide.

The remaining children were not in sufficiently critical condition to be flown to Lamar. Around 2:30 p.m. neighbors drove Lena and Carl Huffaker, Eunice and Leland Frost, Clara Smith, and Maxine Brown to the Holly Hotel and to the homes of Holly physicians F. E. Casburn and John Neinhuis for evaluation. Evelyn and Ome Untiedt napped in a bright, cheery room at the Holly home of Irvin and Bessie Romer, then snacked on chocolate milk and sweet rolls.[24]

As soon as physicians at the Maxwell Hospital saw the worrisome frostbite on Alice, Blanche, and Rosemary, they called the Holly doctors and demanded to see the other children as well. Even Laura and Max Huffaker, so unscathed that they had gone home with their father, were driven to the Maxwell Hospital on the doctors' orders. Evelyn and Ome left the comfortable Romer home reluctantly for the hospital. By now the roads were clear enough to traverse easily.

On their rented farm near Hartman, Bill and Ora Smith reeled with the news they received from their son Walter, who had just returned from the Reinert farmhouse near the Pleasant Hill School. Their sons, Ralph and Louis, had stayed safely home from school during the worst blizzard of their young lives, but the bus that their dear Clara rode had been stranded and it was miraculous that she was alive. Their daughter Nora, who rode the west-side bus and was living with the Albert Crum family, was perfectly safe. But Clara! They would visit her as soon as possible. The rumor was that most of the children's hands and feet would have to be amputated. Bill Smith saddled up a horse and headed for the Reinert home, but by the time he arrived the children were already gone.

❄✳❄✳❄

Carl Miller's body most certainly lay somewhere under the sinking sun while Ralph Lucius and his fellow searchers tramped across many square miles of snow looking for it. They were prepared for the reality that it might take hours, even days, to locate the driver. They had been out all afternoon, and darkness would arrive within the hour. It was Saturday evening, March 28, and everyone presumed that Miller would not be found alive. The men wondered where Miller thought he was when he set out from the stranded bus. He could not have gone much farther than a mile in any direction—with such a wicked wind chill he would have frozen to death before reaching any farmhouse. Plus, he set out from the bus soon after dawn on Friday, already exhausted from lack of sleep and food. The blowing snow would have obscured his vision. The searchers now spread out in a circle. Snowdrifts still had not melted, but there were wide areas blown clean. The men spied an occasional frozen jackrabbit, but no human body. Miller could have fallen into a snowdrift, a ditch, or one of the ubiquitous splits in the dry prairie. If so, his body would not be visible unless someone literally stumbled over it.

After hours of scanning the landscape, Lucius got in his car and drove farther south along the Holly–Towner road. Someone shouted to him that to proceed too far would be pointless, but Lucius wondered if perhaps the other searchers were underestimating Miller's stamina. Miller probably would have followed a fence line or a barrow ditch, Lucius thought. So he proceeded along the fence southward. About three miles south of the bus, the fence turned east. If Miller had been hoping to come upon a house, he may have followed the turn. Near the crest, about a half mile from the road, a dark object caught Lucius's eye. He got out of his car and walked closer. It was the body of a man on its back, frozen solid. Its head was bare and its suitcoat unbuttoned.[25] Lucius gazed at the pitiably outstretched arms and swollen face. Miller had continued to grasp the barbed-wire fence even after his hands lost sensation. His gloves still covered his fingers, but the palms of his hands were left exposed where the sharp wire had torn through. His flesh was raw and blood had dried in the gashes. Lucius turned to alert the others that the final victim of the Pleasant Hill death bus had been located.

CHAPTER SEVEN

"Daddy Is Coming"

THE CHILDREN AWOKE in clean, cool hospital rooms in Lamar, forty-nine miles west of that horrid place near the Pleasant Hill School. It was Sunday morning, March 29, 1931. For most, this was the first time in a hospital, and they were reacting with varying emotions.

Smiling and reassuring physicians and nurses poured hot soup and chilled fruit juice down them, fluffed their pillows, and adjusted their blankets. In this soothing atmosphere, away from the bitter cold, the children finally began to react to the physical and emotional trauma that their brains had not allowed them to experience earlier. Nobody warned them that the thawing and healing would be so intensely painful. As seven-year-old Leland Frost's nerves awoke to the pain of his frostbite and his emotions to the previous horror, he became hysterical. He screamed in terror throughout that night and for many nights to come. His father and a nun had to hold him down in bed to prevent self-injury.

As the children awoke, they were told that Mary Louise Miller and Arlo Untiedt had died at the Reinert farm, bringing the death toll to five, plus Carl Miller. Though some of them already knew or suspected it, the certainty stunned them. The horror was not over simply because they were in a safe building. Ome Untiedt, who had been so close to his younger brother, refused to talk about Arlo. They were also told that Maude Moser and Franz Freiday were safe; they had made it to the boarding homes without injury.

Dave and Nellie Stonebraker received a telephone message from the hospital that their ten-year-old daughter, Blanche, would probably follow her sister Louise into death. The doctors and nurses were doing all they could, the caller assured them, but her tissue was badly damaged and her vital signs weak. Dave Stonebraker had seen Blanche's glazed stare and ice-covered hair. Her spirit was stronger than her sister's had been, however, so if anything would help, that would.

Charley Huffaker, the twelve-year-old friend of Bryan Untiedt, did not particularly mind being in the hospital. Neither he nor Bryan was in danger of losing limbs (though Bryan's feet suffered mild frostbite), but the physicians believed it prudent to observe them closely for signs of developing pneumonia. When Charley least expected it, memories of the deep chill that had invaded his body recurred, and he had to remind himself repeatedly that the ordeal was over. He was all right, and none of his brothers or sisters had died. They were safe now. Still, he worried about his sister Alice—he heard up and down the hospital hallway that her partially frozen hands and lower legs would probably have to be amputated. He knew his parents worried also, but they kept their fears from their children.

This was a comfortable place to rest—and quiet during the times reporters and photographers were not there. Saturday evening, when the children had only been hospitalized for a few hours, reporters canvassed the hospital talking to the physicians and nurses. Doctors C. T. Knuckey, R. J. Rummell, J. S. Hasty, and Napoleon Burnett tended to the children. Seven or more nurses and hospital superintendent Marie Wadham administered serum to prevent pneumonia and wrapped gauze around frozen hands, feet, and faces. Reporters interviewed Bryan Untiedt, probably because he was a glib, older child. Bud Untiedt sat in Bryan's room. Charley Huffaker, whose room was adjacent to Bryan's, heard Bud responding to the reporters' questions as often as did Bryan, even answering questions addressed to Bryan. One reporter stopped in Charley's room to ask him a few questions, but as the children would learn, Bryan was being singled out by the press as a hero.

Alice Huffaker could scarcely remember anything that took place from the time she was removed from the bus until Saturday night at the hospital. That night a nurse cut blisters from her hands and feet, and Alice saw purple skin stretched over feet so misshapen they did not seem to be hers. When the nurse finished, she swathed Alice's stiff hands in layers of bandages. Everything in her body ached. Alice heard her brother Charley in the next room talking briefly to a reporter about the incident, and through the half-open door she glimpsed one of the older Brown sons visiting his sisters Rosemary and Maxine. She closed her eyes then and opened them the next day to the mid-morning Sunday sunshine outside the hospital window. The nurse brought some porridge and spoon-fed her. Alice, the second-oldest and most self-assured child in her family, was being fed like a baby. Though the nurses assured her that she was very much alive, her brain felt dead.

Dr. Napoleon Burnett, the physician in charge of treating the children, had recently completed a course on frostbite care. When the children arrived in Lamar by airplane, Dr. Burnett met them at the airstrip. He later told the *Lamar Daily News* that treatment consisted of "putting the patients to bed in cool, well-ventilated rooms, administration of drugs and stimulants. The frozen parts were first washed and cleansed with grain alcohol then the application of antiseptic dressings, iodized oil, and mercurochrome ointment. Then the frozen parts were carefully placed at rest in the most comfortable positions, using great care to avoid traumatizing or injuring the frozen tissue. All rubbing, massage, or manipulation of any kind were absolutely prohibited, no hot water bottles or external heat of

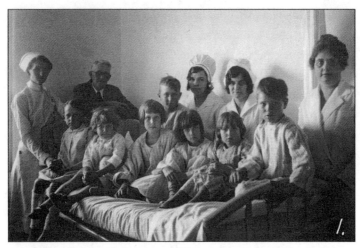

J. H. Ward of the *Lamar Daily News* assembled survivors and hospital personnel for a series of photos at the Maxwell Hospital. Front, from left: Leland Frost, Laura Huffaker, Evelyn Untiedt, Maxine Brown, Lena and Carl Huffaker. Rear: Julia Rybak, Charles Maxwell, Max Huffaker, two unidentified nurses, and Marie Wadham.

any kind permitted to the frozen parts." In addition, he prescribed unlimited hot liquids and fruit juice, and a "stimulating nourishing diet." Two children—he did not specify which ones and the children never knew what their treatment consisted of—experienced pain so severe when their limbs began to thaw that he prescribed opiates.

The doctor went on to explain that the manipulation of frozen body parts damaged blood vessels and tissue. Because such treatment was administered at the Reinert ranch, it was nothing short of miraculous that no amputations were required. Dr. Burnett's treatment seemed to be ultimately responsible for saving limbs and digits, and by Tuesday he knew that the risk of gangrene was passing and that the chances of pneumonia were decreasing significantly. As the days went by and the children improved, he pronounced that they would all survive. So while five youngsters had contracted such severe hypothermia that they died, none of

the survivors—for reasons beyond understanding then or later—
lost even a finger or toe to frostbite.

Eunice Frost's frostbitten feet had to be propped, uncovered, on
a pile of blankets. Once, she made the mistake of covering them with
a sheet and had to quickly snatch it away. The light cotton cloth felt
like a fallen tree on her swollen feet. She awoke several times each
night in a panic, crying, "Get off my feet!" Then she looked down at
her bare, uncovered feet and realized that the pain was dreadful even
without anything touching the nerves. It was a constant sensation of
thousands of needles pricking her skin.

Eunice worried about her little brother, Leland, down the hall,
who was such an innocent child. He did well in school—that was
partly to Eunice's credit. Before he started school, she taught him to
count and to say the alphabet. They used to sit in the granary before
dinner reciting. She hoped he would recover from his night terrors
and that life would return to normal. She hoped they would be able
to escape from this confounded hospital, and that the pain would
someday vanish, and that they could return to life as it was before. A
year after the incident, Eunice's father, Claude Frost, would admit to
her that he, who had never been religious, prayed the day he saw his
traumatized children in the hospital: "Lord, if none of the kids lose a
toe or finger or any limbs, I'll serve you."

Blanche Stonebraker, who defied the doctor's initial prognosis
of certain death, heard two nurses discussing a plan to see a moving
picture. She wanted to go, too, because she had never seen one. One
nurse joked, "Let's stick you in my pocket and you can go with us."
But Blanche had to stay in the hospital through the week until her
limbs thawed enough that her mother could care for her.

As Rosemary Brown's feet thawed and new skin began to grow,
old skin peeled off in large sheets. Her sister Maxine was horrified to
see the entire outer layer of skin covering Rosemary's big toe come
off in one piece, but Rosemary dully accepted it. It helped that the

nurses treated her kindly. But every time Rosemary saw how distraught her mother was, particularly over the death of little Bobbie, she felt guilty. Bobbie was her little brother, after all. There must have been *something* she could have done to save him. His death, she felt, was largely her fault.

Lena Huffaker and Maxine Brown, lonely for their parents and weary of the hospital, longed to go home. Every day they begged eight-year-old Laura Huffaker—who, incredibly, was not even nipped with frostbite—to ask for their release, but her timid pleas did no good. All the children would remain in the hospital the entire week, in case pneumonia developed. Kenneth Johnson's father, Ernie, also spent time in the Maxwell Hospital to prevent developing pneumonia, which threatened him after he spent hours in the cold searching for the bus that contained his dying son.

Some parents directed their fury toward the teachers who had sent the children into the blizzard. Franz Freiday responded publicly in a March 30 *Rocky Mountain News* story headlined: "Teacher Takes 'Blame' in School Bus Tragedy." Freiday defended the decision made jointly with Maude Moser, claiming that after discussion, any "sensible" person would have reached the same conclusion: It would be better for the children to be at home during the storm rather than marooned in a schoolhouse. Freiday also stood up for Moser, taking a share of the responsibility rather than letting it be placed solely upon her. Moser declined comment, allowing her colleague to speak with the *News* and other news organizations on her behalf.

That same day, the education committee of the Colorado Legislature considered a bill requiring that telephones be installed in all country schools and that blankets or heaters and canned food be stored in all school buses. The bill passed unanimously on second reading. Of course, few rural homes of the early 1930s Depression were equipped with telephones, so a teacher could not contact a home to cancel classes even if the school had a telephone. Still, contact could be made with a sheriff or with school administrators, provided that phone lines remained up. Newspapers reported other cases of teachers and children being stranded in schoolhouses around the state, but a tragedy similar to Pleasant Hill's was averted because they had remained inside.

Kiowa County Coroner H. G. Hopkins visited the death scene Sunday, March 29, from his office in the county seat of Eads, fifty-three miles west of the Pleasant Hill district. He announced the next day that an inquest would be unnecessary because it was obvious that accidental freezing had caused the deaths. No agency ever investigated the tragedy.

Hopkins was not the only visitor to Pleasant Hill. In addition to the Colorado and Kansas newspaper reporters, newsreel photographers from Oklahoma City and Chicago traveled to Lamar, Holly, and the Pleasant Hill community. Reporters of every media venue recognized the enormous public concern for these young storm victims. Citizens who owned radios could tune in to news programs on the nearest station for updates on the frozen children.

The Church and Sharp Funeral Home in Lamar arranged a group funeral service and the A. A. Morich Mortuary of Holly prepared the coffins. The memorial service was scheduled to be held in the armory, Holly's largest building, followed by a burial in Holly's town cemetery.

On Tuesday, the last day of March and only six days after the Pleasant Hill bus lurched into the snow, approximately a thousand mourners arrived from towns and farms throughout southeastern Colorado and western Kansas. All businesses in Holly closed for the afternoon, and area schools canceled classes. Friends, relatives, and curiosity seekers began entering the armory at 10:00 a.m. for the 1:30 p.m. service. The one-room armory, big enough for a full basketball court and a few bleachers, could barely hold six hundred people. Bleachers usually accommodating basketball spectators were now reserved for the immediate families of the deceased, and the remaining seats filled early. The overflow crowd congregated in the muddy street and in the alley behind the armory.

Inside, flowers decorated the six open coffins. Before the service, a continuous line of mourners trudged past the caskets, paying last respects to Carl Miller, who lost his life seeking help; to his little girl, Mary Louise, who was so proud to be the bus driver's daughter; to Arlo Untiedt, who was never apart from his brother Ome; to the little adopted Kenneth Johnson, who without siblings was the responsibility of all the children on the bus; to Bobbie Brown, who hated being cold and wet; and to Louise Stonebraker, who convinced her mother that she should wear her light sweater to school.

The service began at 1:30 p.m. Governor Billy Adams had sent letters of condolence to the grieving families, and the one addressed to Geneva Miller was read aloud at the beginning of the service:

Dear Mrs. Miller:

It was with a great deal of sorrow that I, as well as the other citizens of the state, learned of the recent tragedy which befell your beloved husband and daughter. His acts of heroism will live thru [sic] many generations thruout [sic] the entire state and nation. In [sic] behalf of the citizens of Colorado, I extend my deepest sympathy in your hour of bereavement.

> *Sincerely,*
> *William H. Adams*
> *Governor of Colorado*

Though Geneva appreciated the governor's sympathy, his letter did little to comfort her.

The memorial at the Holly Cemetery is surrounded by the six who perished in the blizzard. Some of the survivors chose to be buried alongside them when their time came.

Ministers from four churches shared the duties of eulogizing the children: I. J. Gorby, Presbyterian; C. H. Foster, Baptist; E. L. Butler, Methodist; and A. R. Nichols, Pentecostal. A twelve-person choir sang "In the Garden," "Precious Jewels," "From Every Stormy Wind That Blows," and "Asleep in Jesus." The Reverend Nichols read verses from John 14 and Revelations 21. The Reverend Butler read the obituaries of the deceased, then offered a prayer. The organ and piano concluded the service with a solemn dirge. As mourners filed out of the armory, those who had not viewed the bodies walked past the caskets. Grieving parents touched their dead children's faces one final time, and then the caskets were closed and removed to the waiting hearses.

Classmates of the deceased children watched the bereaved families cry. The Johnsons, who were so grateful for the opportunity to adopt Kenneth, were again childless. Wanda Crum, the ten-year-old who rode the west-side car to the Pleasant Hill School, could not

The monument at the Holly Cemetery honors the victims of
the March 26–27, 1931, blizzard. The structure was dedicated
on October 7, 1931, with many townspeople in attendance.

believe that only last week Arlo Untiedt, Mary Louise Miller, Kenneth Johnson, and Bobbie Brown had been sitting in her classroom. Only one week ago they were dashing around the schoolyard with their siblings and classmates. And now she would never see them again. Wanda's father, Arna, gripped her shoulder. Hordes of people crowded into the armory, and Arna did not want to lose Wanda or her siblings in the throng. He told her that he was enormously grateful that they happened to live on the west side of the school district, and that her driver had happened to find a house—his cousin's house—for them to stay in during the blizzard. She knew that he was guiltily thankful to be attending the funeral of other people's children. Clara Smith's eleven-year-old brother, Louis, attended the funeral with his mother and older brother, Ed. He, too, was stunned to think that only last week he had been playing with his friends in the schoolyard and now was gazing in disbelief at their swollen faces in caskets. Death apparently stole people arbitrarily. Why these children that he knew? And why was Clara spared?

Spectators tramped along the road leading to Holly's cemetery, a mile northeast of downtown. Among the crowd were a movie crew, reporters and photographers, and nearly fifty close relatives of the deceased. Two Colorado National Guard airplanes flew overhead scattering flowers courtesy of Fred Bonfils of *The Denver Post*, Governor Adams, the family of A. E. Humphreys, Jr., the Park Floral Company, the Cooper Flower Store, and the Elitch Gardens greenhouses—all in Denver. Captain Eddie Brooks, who piloted the Humphreys plane to the Reinert ranch, flew one of the planes. The other was piloted by one of Colorado's famed aviators of the time, Major Carlos Reavis of the National Guard. A third plane, carrying reporters from the *Rocky Mountain News*, was piloted by Walter Higley. Flight time from Denver to Holly, depending on the weather, was approximately one and a half hours. *Denver Post* reporter C. L. "Poss" Parsons accompanied fellow *Post* reporter Fred Warren, who broke the story.

As Louise Stonebraker's casket was lowered into the ground, someone in the crowd murmured, "Today would have been Louise's fourteenth birthday."

✳✳✳✳✳

Because of their continued convalescence in the Maxwell Hospital, none of the injured children was able to attend the service. Rosemary Brown, for one, would always regret the lack of closure, the lost opportunity to grieve with her family and community for her brother and classmates. If only she did not feel so terribly responsible for Bobbie's death. Her sister Maxine felt cheated that Bobbie had simply gone to sleep, and that she did not have a chance to say good-bye. They played together every day, then suddenly he was gone. Alice Huffaker also wished she could have been at the funeral, so that the deaths would have felt real.

Bryan Untiedt was the only survivor to receive a letter from the governor of Colorado. One of the Colorado National Guard planes that flew over the funeral made a special trip to deliver the letter to the hospital:

Master Bryan Untiedt
Maxwell Hospital, Lamar, Colorado

Dear Bryan:

The State of Colorado extends to you its whole-hearted thanks for your valiant and heroic deeds of the last week. To the parents and friends of the playmates whose lives you saved, you have brought untold Joy and blessings. You have performed acts of heroism which will be remembered for many generations thruout [sic] the entire state and nation. In [sic] behalf of the citizens of Colorado, I extend grateful thanks.

Sincerely,
William H. Adams
Governor of Colorado

Ernest Johnson, recovering in the Lamar hospital from exposure, wrote to the editor of the *Lamar Daily News* on April 3. He lamented that after looking for the bus all day Friday, by the time the children were rescued it was too late. "I always told my little son that I would come to him in time of trouble no matter what happened and he kept telling the children, 'My daddy is coming.' They told me that was the last words he said—'Daddy is coming.' Fate kept me from reaching them in time, for he died about an hour before we found them."

CHAPTER EIGHT

And a Hero Is Created

❄❄❄❄

"*POST* PLANE RUSHES SURVIVORS of Bus Tragedy to Hospital" was the headline greeting *Denver Post* readers on Sunday, March 29, 1931. The *Post* opened its Pleasant Hill coverage: "It is a story of pathos, of fortitude, of endurance, of bravery, of death, and the love of the human being for life. It is a story that tugs at the heartstrings and leaves its hearers to stand and wonder how human beings could endure what these children endured and live to tell of it."

Had the *Post* continued with restraint, its 316,000 Sunday readers across Colorado and the Rocky Mountain West would have received a fairly accurate and unsensationalized account of the Pleasant Hill tragedy. But with publisher Fred Bonfils in command, accompanying the story was a large front-page photograph of Bryan Untiedt and a caption proclaiming him the "Hero of Bus Tragedy," and continuing:

> *Bryan Untiedt, thirteen years old, who risked his own life in an attempt to save the nineteen children who were marooned with him on a storm-swept highway near Towner, Colorado, Thursday and Friday during the worst spring blizzard eastern Colorado has experienced in years. He literally stripped himself to his under-clothing to give his outer garments to smaller children. His heroic*

work in keeping the other youngsters awake saved many lives.
Bryan is shown here all bundled up to be removed to Lamar in
the A. E. Humphreys, Jr. plane which was dispatched to Towner
by The Denver Post.

Bryan Untiedt took off his clothing to save the little children?
parents wondered. Their children had not spoken of such a thing.
When Dave Stonebraker heard about the *Post*'s statement, he suddenly understood reporter Fred Warren's words overheard two
nights before: Bryan Untiedt had been chosen as the single person
on the bus who had performed extraordinary lifesaving acts—as if
each child's survival were not an extraordinary event in itself. No one
told Dave Stonebraker that Bryan gave anyone his clothing. When
Stonebraker first entered the bus, he saw that all the children had
removed their coats and some had taken off hats and gloves as well.
That was, he now knew, because they felt a growing warmness as
death approached. And Stonebraker certainly did not notice Bryan
Untiedt wearing only his underwear in the death bus.

Clara Smith supposed that reporters sought out Bryan over the
other children because he was talkative, personable, and related stories well. Alice Huffaker knew that not only was Bryan naturally glib,
but he was also the least frozen of the older children. Much of the
publicity, therefore, centered on Bryan Untiedt.[26]

On April 2, a week after the bus came to its final stop, *The
Denver Post* and KOA radio in Denver broadcast a special fifteen-
minute program designed for and beamed to the hospitalized
children. Yarn spinner Scotty Williams told an original bedtime
story and Charles J. Scheuerman's thirteen-piece orchestra played
a few tunes. Some of the children did not have radios at home, so
hearing a radio program was a rare opportunity. The *Post* claimed
that in anticipation of the afternoon program, "pains in frozen
arms and legs were forgotten" and that the children "could talk

of nothing but the broadcast." Frances "Pinky" Wayne, the *Post*'s famed gossip writer, addressed the Pleasant Hill victims over KOA:

> *Hello, you dear young heroes of the storm! I am speaking for Frederick G. Bonfils, publisher of* The Denver Post, *who—through the courtesy of Mr. and Mrs. A. E. Humphreys—rushed the airplane to your rescue, and for all those in Colorado and elsewhere who are filled with pride that in you they have discovered again the qualities of heart and spirit that helped win and build this beautiful west of ours. Isn't it wonderful, Children, that, standing here in Denver in the beautiful studio of KOA, I can, through the miracle we call radio, talk to you in your flower-and-toy-filled rooms at the hospital in Lamar as though nothing divided us? For a little while the people of Colorado and of the entire country saw only black tragedy in the thing that happened to you last Thursday. We trembled for you. Then, through the darkness, came something fine and splendid, for we had found fifteen boys and girls who know how to meet emergencies, who can stand together in the face of frightful odds,* take punishment with a smile *[emphasis added], and have proved that victory can be won through the exercise of self-control and obedience. What you children mean to Colorado cannot be measured by any rule. The people love and are proud of you. They are going to watch you and your gallant leader, Bryan Untiedt, as you grow into manhood and womanhood. The Denver Post will keep track of you. If you come to Denver, the latchstring is out for each and all. Meantime, we congratulate Bryan on his birthday anniversary with best wishes and many happy returns of the day. And for you all, good luck! Faces front!*

After the broadcast, the *Post* positively glowed: "To the children, this special radio program was worth all the suffering they endured in the stalled bus." Rosemary Brown, for one, was not wearing a smile, did not "feel fine and splendid," and further, could not even stand up. Her pain was not "forgotten." In fact, to the contrary, as her frozen feet were beginning to heal, and as the process continued, the pain increased. The fifteen-minute radio program was not worth the suffering she endured and not worth watching her little brother fall dead at her feet. She and the others who suffered from frostbite had to prop their feet on piles of blankets. The radio broadcast was one of many diversions Rosemary had to tolerate. By day, the children, who all remained in the hospital under careful surveillance for pneumonia, appeared to be healing. But at night, the horrors returned in dreams. Events such as this broadcast diverted their attention for only minutes. Years later, Rosemary had little recollection of the radio program.

The *Post*, it seemed to the people in southeastern Colorado, patronizingly interpreted the tragedy as a blessing in disguise for these farm-bred children; an incident from which they could learn a lesson about life, and garner accolades, fame, and cash donations along the way. The youngsters in their beds in the Maxwell Hospital, however, simply wanted life to return to normal—though it never could because their friends and siblings were dead, and most of their parents refused to discuss the event. They were not allowed to grieve. It was believed that the less the parents discussed the horrors of the cold, pain, and death, the less the children would dwell on them and the sooner they would feel normal. This was the accepted and prevailing method of contending with emotional pain.

The Pleasant Hill bus catastrophe provided Fred Bonfils with his biggest story (read it: greatest circulation opportunity) in a long spell. The *Rocky Mountain News*, the rival of the *Post* in Denver, also reported on the school bus tragedy but was clearly and continually outhustled by the larger and more brash *Post*. After the March 31 funerals, in fact, the *News* did not mention the recuperating children. The *Post* kept reporters on the scene and used its front page daily until April 21—fully twenty-five days after the story broke. From March 28 to April 20, the *Post* devoted a total of 1,643 column inches to the Pleasant Hill story, while the *News* allowed 621 column inches. Not only did the *Post* offer the lengthiest accounts of the already well-established Pleasant Hill saga, but as time would prove, the *Post* helped shape the lives of the tragedy's survivors.

On April 2, the American Legion in Lamar staged a boxing benefit, with proceeds going to families of the children. Spectators filled the Lamar armory; the event netted a sizable $700. The *Lamar Daily News* formed a benefit committee, composed of Jesse Johnston, mayor and hospital owner Charles Maxwell, and *Lamar Daily News* publisher Fred M. Betz, to decide how much money would go to each family. The committee would consider the finances of survivors' and victims' families, so that the money could be distributed fairly.

The Denver Post took partial credit for the boxing event, but did not mention that the benefit was cosponsored by the *Lamar Daily News*, the American Legion, and Les Showers's Amateur Athletic Union (AAU) organization. Neither did the *Post* consistently note charitable acts by *anybody* but itself. The First National Bank of Wichita, for example, sent a $500 check for a relief fund to be administered by the Holly Commercial Club. The *Montrose Press*, in western Colorado, offered to help raise money for Geneva Miller. KGEK, a radio station in Yuma, Colorado, raised $900 for the survivors, allocated as such: $300 to start a construction fund for a monument to the victims, $300 to the children who survived, earmarked for new clothes, and $300 to Geneva Miller. Schoolchildren in Eads later contributed $3 to the fund.

The Denver Post did not just report on Pleasant Hill; it injected itself into the story. Dispatching the Humphreys Fokker to the Reinert farm and transporting some of the afflicted to Lamar was

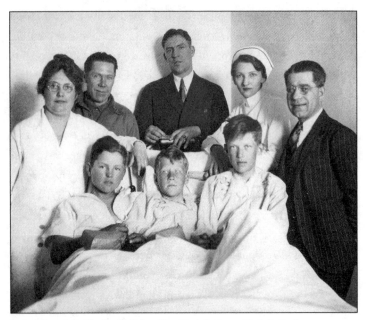

In bed, from left: Charley Huffaker, Ome Untiedt, Bryan Untiedt. Back center: heavyweight boxer Angus Snyder of Dodge City, Kansas, who headlined a benefit boxing match in Lamar. Around him are Marie Wadham, pilot Jack Hart, Julia Rybak, and Jerry Jolton of the American Legion.

the *Post*'s first and most direct involvement. But the paper came up with other angles, each receiving notable attention in its news columns: "*Post* to Give Benefit Show for Bus Victims' Families" was the headline on April 2. P. R. "Reddy" Gallagher of the *Post*'s sports department organized a wrestling benefit staged in Denver City Auditorium on Monday, April 6. With a top admission price of a dollar, the show attracted 3,500 people. Overhead costs were donated, and companies bought blocks of seats for their employees. *The Denver Post* assured its readers that every cent of the $2,136 collected would go to the survivors and their families and to Geneva Miller. The paper reported that as of April 9, "*Post* Raises $4,500 to Aid Bus Survivors and Families" and the much smaller subhead read, "Total Contributions from All Sources Amount to $7,500." The article mentioned that individuals across the country had sent cash directly to the survivors, and therefore might not have been recorded with running totals. The $7,500 represented an estimated 10,000 contributors, many of whom were schoolchildren literally donating pennies.

However, bus coverage did not enhance *Post* circulation. Daily circulation in March, prior to the bus incident, averaged 189,200, with a Sunday average of 315,148. The daily circulation in April declined to an average of 185,609. The Sunday numbers grew ever so slightly to 315,461.

The story of Pleasant Hill's children, broadcast by radio stations throughout the world, provoked extraordinary response. Newspaper photographers (primarily J. H. Ward of the *Lamar Daily News*) grouped together children, hospital administrators, hospital owner Charles Maxwell, nurses, a boxer who fought during a benefit for them, and even the teachers Maude Moser and Franz Freiday. The pictures appeared in newspapers throughout the United States. Sympathetic people as far away as Germany mailed letters, gifts, and cash to the Maxwell Hospital in Lamar. Lamar businesses donated clothing, and a Lamar bank gave the survivors coin banks shaped like its building. (New clothes and real folding money for children whose wardrobes had always been homemade hand-me-downs and whose own money was counted in pennies and nickels!) Lamar citizens donated angel food cakes, books, pajamas, bloomers, coats, and other clothing. For Easter, the final day of their hospital stay, each of the children received an enormous box of candy, courtesy of Joseph Jacobs, manager of Denver's famous Baur's Confectionary, and—who else? —*The Denver Post. The Post* duly noted its gift in its columns, concluding that "no millionaire could have bought any finer Easter presents for the little folk."

Whatever self-aggrandizement the big *Denver Post* afforded itself over the Pleasant Hill tragedy, the daily paper situated nearest the bus incident felt compelled to point out its own efforts. The *Lamar Daily News* on March 30, said:

Because of the fact that the Lamar Daily News *was the nearest daily newspaper to the tragedy, requests have been pouring into this office since Friday morning for information, pictures, and news stories. Great news stories only become great when it is discovered that the news event has "clicked" with the interest in the mind of the newsreader. The man on the street, the woman in the home, children, everybody, was interested in the fate of the unfortunate Kiowa County school kiddies, the bus driver, the teachers, and everything connected with the affair. Newspaper readers on the streets of New York City knew of the event before half the citizens of Prowers or Kiowa counties knew what had taken place. After the first news was given to the world by the United Press Association, of which the* Daily News *is a member, in came the requests from New York City, Chicago, San Francisco, Kansas City, Denver, Tulsa, and other population centers. By Saturday night the request for facts had mounted into a flood, and information compiled by the* Daily News—*with three men at the scene of the tragedy for five hours, covering every phase of the event and making pictures of all items of interest—went forth to be the feature story on the front page of practically every Sunday metropolitan paper in the United States. The suffering of little children appeals to the most hardened individual.*

Geneva Miller, a hardy and able rural woman, could not maintain the farm and raise her surviving child, Louis, without financial help. *The Denver Post* established a fund in her name and contributed the initial fifty dollars; individual donors, whose names and dollar contributions were listed in the *Post*, donated from one dollar to ten dollars or more. The fund grew to $2,466.22. Because Carl Miller was employed by the school system, Geneva also received a death compensation of $3,606.25, payable at fifty dollars a month. With the *Post* money, Geneva bought an automobile and paid debts on her cattle. The insurance money supported her and Louis until she remarried in June 1932.

On Friday, April 3, the children of Pleasant Hill celebrated Bryan Untiedt's thirteenth birthday in the basement dining room of the Maxwell Hospital. Afterward, they were bundled up and carried to waiting automobiles to attend a movie at Lamar's Isis Theater—the first movie ever for most of them—called *Big Money*, starring Eddie Quillan. Bryan himself would be featured in a newsreel film shot that weekend by Hearst Metrotone News.

Motion picture newsreel coverage was a point of disagreement among some of the parents. During a discussion regarding such filming, Dave Stonebraker, realizing that images of his daughter Blanche would be shown in theaters nationwide, demanded that the parents be remunerated for their children's appearances in the news clips. Newsreel photographers Eddie Morrison and M. P. Gleason declared that they had already arranged the filming with Franz Freiday and Claude Frost. Bud Untiedt advised Stonebraker not to argue. Media coverage seemed ceaseless.[27]

KOA, the NBC affiliate in Denver, surpassed the *Post*'s radio show of the previous week by broadcasting a live program, featuring the children's voices, from the Maxwell Hospital. Because all the children but Clara Smith had returned home on April 5, local citizens, at the behest of the *Lamar Daily News*, transported the children and their families to Lamar for the April 9 broadcast.[28] Hospital personnel and Charles Maxwell crowded into Clara Smith's room with the children. After being introduced, the children greeted the radio listeners and recited jingles. Bryan Untiedt, Clara Smith, and Eunice

Frost related brief tales of their experiences on the bus. Dr. Burnett explained his methods of treating the children, and then Franz Friday spoke on taking precautionary measures against storms. The program concluded with Bryan Untiedt's harmonica rendition of "*Oh, Dem Golden Slippers.*"

NBC also donated $500 to the children's families, which was divided among them.

Indisputably, the efforts of *The Denver Post* financially benefited the surviving children of the Pleasant Hill school bus tragedy. But also because of the *Post*, certain hardships were imposed on them, particularly upon Bryan Untiedt. The *Post* reported on April 3 that base commander C. R. Howland of Fort Francis E. Warren in Cheyenne, Wyoming, recommended that young Bryan receive a Carnegie Medal. Howland wrote to Bonfils proposing that this highest of US civilian honors should go to the lad who saved the lives of his classmates. The next day, Bryan received a long-distance telephone call from President Herbert Hoover's secretary. Bryan's mother, by the sides of her children in the Maxwell Hospital, took the call, which was an invitation for Bryan to visit the president in Washington, D.C. Bryan's parents agreed to let him make the trip.

Bryan's sudden fame hit the Untiedt family unexpectedly. Still in shock over the death of their son Arlo, the parents found themselves dealing with big-city reporters and representatives of the president of the United States! Hazel Untiedt had a brood of five to care for, including baby Ruth Elaine and sickly Virgil; their house girl Clara Smith lay injured in the hospital and unable to help with chores; and the work on the farm did not cease so they could grieve the loss of little Arlo. So much was happening all at one time.

And it was happening to Bryan as well. As the eldest of the Untiedt offspring, he had always been responsible for watching out for his siblings, Virgil, Evelyn, Arlo, Ome, and recently, Ruth Elaine.

He had done the labor of a grown man since the age of eight when he began driving a team of horses in the fields. His childhood consisted of adult responsibilities. And now, on the cusp of his thirteenth birthday, this horrifying event somehow foisted upon him another colossal responsibility: dealing with the status of hero. Newspapers around the country wanted the name of this ordinary country boy in their headlines, so he talked to them. He talked to the reporters, and he would now talk to the president of the United States and to grown-ups who had never harvested crops or milked cows or been caught in a killer blizzard.

But after all of the pandemonium ceased, Bryan Untiedt largely refused to discuss the Pleasant Hill bus tragedy ever again.

CHAPTER NINE

Going Home

FRED BONFILS INTENDED to keep the Pleasant Hill story alive for as long as he could continue devising new angles. On April 5, his newspaper headline announced, "Bus Survivors Will Be Guests for Week of *The Denver Post*." This was Bonfils's most extravagant grandstand ploy of all: an all-expense-paid railroad trip to Denver for the survivors and their families, as well as for Geneva Miller and Dr. Burnett and his family. Now curious *Post* readers, tantalized by the previous week of nonstop coverage, could see the survivors in person—never mind that the victims were still ailing, physically and emotionally. The public, the *Post* knew, needed distractions from the Depression's everyday rigors.

The *Rocky Mountain News* viewed with disdain the Bonfils sideshow built around the Pleasant Hill survivors. The smaller and far less flashy *News* accused the *Post* of being noisy and exploitative, and denied Bonfils any credit by headlining the trip as a "Week of Thrills on Invitation of Mayor [Ben] Stapleton." An April 8 *News* editorial, headlined "Best Praise of Heroism Is Service," pointed out that Bonfils's unabashed glorification of the children was overblown and not the most compassionate use of the power of a news organization:

> *Sometimes the finest tributes are those paid quietly and unostentatiously—with acts rather than words, and service instead of noise.*

This thought arises as various plans for honoring the children in the . . . school bus tragedy go forward. After all, there is only one reason for the honors being paid Bryan Untiedt and the other survivors of the bus tragedy—the desire to express in some way the public's admiration and appreciation of their heroism. They are richly deserving of such approval. But how about a more useful form of approval which has thus far been overlooked—an annuity from the Carnegie Foundation for the wife and infant son of Carl Miller, the bus driver, who gave his life in an effort to save the freezing children? They are the greatest victims of the tragedy, because it cost them their breadwinner. Surely, then, they are most in need of that helpful sort of service which exemplifies the spirit that cost Carl Miller's life.

The News *believes that state and county officials should unite in recommending a hero's pension for the family of the dead bus driver. We shouldn't be carried away by mere noise to the extent of forgetting those left in want as a result of the tragedy. And we hope too, that in the acclaim which will go to Bryan Untiedt and his little companions there will be observed the proprieties so in keeping with the experience for which they are honored. Just as Lindy [aviator Charles Lindbergh] refused to let himself be exploited, so should these young children be saved from the evils of exploitation, from efforts of others to capitalize their deeds.*

Probably nothing would so please these children as to be loved and left in the hearts of their families, with knowledge that the wife and baby of the man who gave his life for them were being fittingly provided for.

Bonfils *had* remembered the plight of Geneva Miller and little Louis. The money raised on their behalf by the *Post* had grown to a sizeable $2,466.22. Yet the *Rocky Mountain News* had a valid point: Underlying the rhetoric of hosting the victims and their families lay the truth that the *Post* was parading the victims around town for its own glory and profit.

The day before their release from the hospital, the children learned of plans being made for their Denver trip the following week. They were simultaneously excited and dubious. Their limbs hurt from the frostbite, and they were still in shock over the deaths of their classmates and siblings, yet how else would they ever get to stay in a first-class hotel in the big city?

No professional counselors or clergy ever spoke with the children of Pleasant Hill about their feelings regarding the tragedy. The prevailing attitude of the time was that the less a grieving person talked about his or her emotions, the faster that individual would heal. No one foresaw that these unconfronted emotions would haunt the Pleasant Hill survivors for their entire lives, manifested through nightmares, unpredictable flashes of panic, and relentless guilt and anger. The parents were also grieving and at a loss to help their children recover from the emotional trauma. They hoped that the distraction of a weeklong trip would help the children forget their pain.

Fern Reinert, whose farmhouse had sheltered the Pleasant Hill youngsters Friday night and Saturday morning a week earlier, had lived temporarily with her own two children at her parents' nearby home. Her husband, Andy, remained at their house until the countryside recovered from the ravages of the storm and Fern returned. When he assessed the state of his livestock, he found two cows whose frozen feet were causing them severe pain; his shotgun ended their suffering.

The following week, neighboring farm women voluntarily went to the Reinert household and cleaned the now grimy concrete-block house. Some boiled the sodden, smelly blankets and clothing and hung the wash out to dry; others cleaned the dishpans that had held snow or food; some scrubbed the furniture and floor. A urine-soaked mattress that had cushioned the children had to be burned. When Fern returned home the first week of April, her house was clean. The only remaining chore was to sand and re-varnish the top of her brand-new sewing machine cabinet that had suffered moisture damage.

Claude and Mary Muriel Frost, the parents of Fern Reinert and of bus survivors Eunice and Leland Frost, sent a letter to the *Lamar Daily News*, which published it on April 9:

WORDS OF APPRECIATION

Having two children who survived the awful bus tragedy of March 26, we feel it our duty to express our thanks and appreciation for the many deeds of kindness and comforting words. We wish to thank the doctors giving first aid and to each and every one braving storm and roads, getting to the children; Mr. Charles Maxwell, who furnished his hospital that the children might be given proper medical attention; the nurses; the owner of the airplanes and the pilots; the people furnishing transportation, and each and everyone from the Pleasant Hill, Towner, Holly, Lamar, and surrounding communities. Words cannot express the gratitude we feel toward each and everyone.

Mr. and Mrs. C. B. Frost and family

Geneva Miller grieved for her husband and daughter—he who had plunged into the blizzard to save the children, and she with the cheerful blue eyes. Now Geneva had only Louis, age one and a half. Though she mentioned to nobody her severe financial strain—worsened by the lack of forthcoming income from Carl's work on the farm—the IGA grocery in Holly quietly sent food and a load of coal to her farm. Geneva was grateful for the humble generosity of the community. She took Louis to her parents' home in Duncan, Oklahoma, to stay for a week. She soon received the enormous $2,465.22 donation from readers of *The Denver Post*. Combined with the school insurance money of $50 per month that she would be paid for Carl's death, Geneva knew she would be able to provide for herself and her son on the farm. While in Oklahoma, she also received a letter of condolence from the White House:

My Dear Mrs. Miller,

I have read with deepest sympathy of your husband and daughter's tragic but heroic death. I am sure you will find comfort in the memory of their self-sacrifice.

Yours faithfully,
Herbert Hoover

After she returned to her farm in Colorado, an aide to Hoover offered Geneva a job at the White House, but she declined. Her life was on the farm in Kiowa County, she told him, and her strongest obligation was to her son. She did not want to be trained to work an eight-hour day in the metropolis and force Louis to spend long hours with a babysitter. When Carl's brother, Ray, offered to help her operate the farm in exchange for a share of the crop, she gladly accepted.

With the exception of Clara Smith, the children were discharged from the hospital on April 5—eight days after their arrival. Clara stayed five days longer because doctors believed that her reproductive organs had been harmed in the blizzard. After their release, Rosemary Brown and Alice Huffaker visited Rosemary's uncle and aunt, Ollie and Emma Brown, in Liberal, Kansas, before embarking on the grand outing to Denver. It was a relief to have a vacation from everyday work and from reporters. Alice and Rosemary longed for a return to normal life, the way it was before Bobbie Brown died, but that would not happen. Ollie and Emma Brown declined to discuss the Pleasant Hill bus incident, but in retrospect Rosemary felt this would have been an ideal time for the girls to share their emotions. Because she had no one to talk to, no one to assure her at this early point that deathly things sometimes happen accidentally, Rosemary began incubating a lifelong guilt that she was responsible for her brother Bobbie's death. Her younger sister, Maxine, was experiencing a similar loss because she and Bobbie had played together often, but the two sisters both tried to put the bus out of their minds by not discussing it.

Alice Huffaker was thinner than before the bus tragedy. Her appetite remained low, and because her hands were wrapped in bandages, others still had to feed her. The skin on her hands began to crack and slough, and one by one, her fingernails fell out. The itching at times was almost unbearable, but there was nothing that could relieve it. Rosemary's feet ached continually; she needed crutches to move about. Because of their injuries, there were not many physical activities the two friends could engage in at the Brown home.

When Clara Smith left the hospital on April 10, she went to her parents' leased home near Hartman, about six miles northwest of Holly, rather than returning to the Untiedt household. Unlike Rosemary and Maxine Brown's parents, who would not bring up the bus topic, Clara's mother and father inquired gently, but Clara often could only cry. She generally preferred to avoid the subject, and soon her parents learned to accommodate her in that regard. They hoped the upcoming trip to Denver would wrench her mind away from the horrors she was trying to forget and fill it with new experiences.

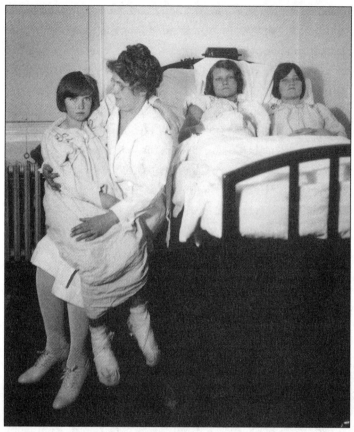

Appearing as if still in shock, Blanche Stonebraker sits on the lap of caregiver Marie Wadham at the Maxwell Hospital. When discharged, Alice Huffaker and Rosemary Brown, here in the bed, would briefly recuperate at the Kansas home of Rosemary's relatives. Note Blanche's heavily bandaged feet.

Clara was featured in a Kodak newsreel shot by E. K. Edwards. He instructed her to ride about on her horse, because the public watching the weekly newsreels in theaters nationwide would be thrilled to see one of the Pleasant Hill survivors in her home environment. It was a novelty for the public, but the media attention made Clara uncomfortable. Photographer Edwards and his theater audiences could not know, as Clara Smith paraded on her horse for them, that she would experience lifelong nightmares about the Pleasant Hill bus.

A girl in Denver circulated a petition among other schoolchildren urging that Clara receive the same recognition—including a Carnegie Medal nomination—as had Bryan Untiedt, who was by now firmly established as the hero of the Pleasant Hill bus. As the oldest girl on the bus, some thought that Clara might have been a hero too, but she dismissed such notions. Nobody was a hero, Clara felt; they were all lucky to have survived. The petition attracted press attention, and some news stories referred to Clara as the "girl hero" of the bus, but Clara was never submitted for consideration of the Carnegie Medal. This was fine with her.

Bryan, Evelyn, and Ome Untiedt returned from the hospital to the two-story home carrying seven boxes of gifts and letters. Evelyn in particular felt happy to be home again after such an extended absence. Bryan received more correspondence and presents than any of the other survivors. The Untiedt parents were relieved to have the three children home again and healthy, but Arlo's absence weighed on them all.

As their automobile, driven by Lee Meadows, publisher of the *Lamar Sparks* newspaper, traveled the dirt road north from Holly toward the Untiedt place, it paused where the Pleasant Hill death bus had stalled. The bus was gone (nobody ever knew what happened to it). Bryan got out and looked around, trying to determine what clues he had missed when he and Clara Smith left the bus and went into the blowing snow. On this clear and sunny day, seven houses were easily visible from where he stood! If only the bitter wind and the snow had let up enough to see . . . *If only their friends could return from the dead.*

The Pleasant Hill school board convened several times during the first half of April, assessing its responsibility in the bus tragedy.

Since most of the Pleasant Hill district's students were recovering from the effects of exposure or were dead, the Pleasant Hill School remained closed until the board could decide the best course of action. On April 11 it decided to reopen school to the west-side pupils. The east-side children would be going to Denver for a week, then back to their homes for further recovery. Even for the east-side students with no lingering physical damage, it hardly made sense to push them to return for the remaining six weeks of school. The April 15 *Lamar Daily News* published a surprisingly abrupt open letter from the board to the community, closing the matter to further discussion:

> *An Open Letter To All Friends and Sympathizers of the Pleasant Hill Blizzard Disaster:*
>
> *By action of the members of the school board in session at Pleasant Hill schoolhouse April 11, it was agreed to reopen the school Monday morning, April 13, with the teachers, Mr. F. R. Freiday and Mrs. Maude E. Moser, again in charge. We wish to thank each and every one for their kindly interest in our great hours of need.*
>
>
>
> *Respectfully signed,*
> *W. A. Bond, President*
> *C. L. Herrick, Secretary*
> *A. C. Reinert, Treasurer*
>
>

Certainly not published was correspondence among school administrators. Pleasant Hill school board secretary, Clarence Herrick, addressed a message dated April 13, 1931, to Alma Vrooman, superintendent of the Kiowa County schools, headquartered in Eads.

Dear Mrs. Vrooman:

You will pardon me I am sure for not answering your letter of 4-4-31 sooner.

In regard to the compensation Ins[urance] for Mrs. Miller, I mailed complete particulars to Denver direct. But I will state that both teachers receive a salary of $105 a month each for a nine month term. Mr. Miller furnished his own School Truck Buss [sic] completely free of any expense to us for $100 a month. Mr. Oscar Reinert furnishes a four door Sedan car entirely at his expense at $69 a month and in the past the compensation Ins[urance] premium has been based on 1/2 as wages and the other 1/2 for thier [sic] rigs where the driver furnishes his own rigs. Since our disaster there has been so much for one to do that I have about needed an asst. Sec. We have had 3 board meetings to ourselves, then 3 board meetings with the teachers then in between times folks of the dis[trict] and hundreds from all around have been calling on me to see what we were [further pages missing from the surviving record].

In a letter dated April 15, 1931, Franz Freiday seemed mostly concerned about whether he, Moser, and driver Oscar Reinert would be paid for the period the school was closed following the tragedy. Revealing that at least one Pleasant Hill board meeting was emotional—perhaps even confrontational—Freiday also suggests that the superintendent, astonishingly, had not visited the Pleasant Hill community following the tragedy:

Holly, Colorado
April 15, 1931

Mrs. Alma Vrooman
Superintendent Public Instruction
Eads, Colorado

Dear Mrs. Vrooman:

Without a great deal of outside persuasion, a compromise was affected [sic] between the teachers and board of directors of Pleasant Hill School.

Things looked dark and gloomy for some time and personalities were aired but no one was seriously injured. After their [the board's] preemptory suggestion of immediate resignation [of Freiday and Moser] had met with a prompt refusal, the members of the board agreed to reopen school for six weeks and to pay the teachers half-time for the weeks March 30 to April 10, as per their contracts. In order to placate the bus driver [Oscar Reinert] it was agreed that the teachers pay $1/3$ each and the district the other $1/3$ of his salary for the two weeks mentioned. By actual figuring the teachers will be short little more than their board bill for the time in question plus $1/3$ of the driver's salary. He was really the one to get the "break." I am glad that it was so easily settled without carrying the affair into greater prominence. I am well satisfied.

School reopened Monday morning with seven pupils in attendance, three new pupils in the district appeared Tuesday and we have the promise of two more pupils Monday of next week. One of them Clara Smith was in the bus tragedy.

Our attendance this week has been hampered by a siege of pink eye in one of the homes.

Hoping that you may be able to visit our school in the near future, and also thanking you for your advice and assistance. I am,

Yours sincerely,
Franz R. Freiday

School closes May 22.[29]

CHAPTER TEN

Remnants of a Disaster

THE EXCITED YOUNGSTERS of Pleasant Hill had seen the giant black locomotives steaming across their prairie, sometimes stopping to unload freight or passengers at the Holly depot before proceeding west to Pueblo or east to Garden City and Dodge City in Kansas. This time they were the ones boarding the Atchison, Topeka & Santa Fe train to Denver, 237 miles to the northwest. Few of the young people had been to Pueblo, let alone Denver. Their entire families were invited on this extravagant jaunt to partake of Denver's finest offerings, including the Lakeside Amusement Park and the Brown Palace—the most famous hotel between Kansas City and the West Coast. Every child was accompanied at least by his or her mother, if not both parents. Even Virgil Untiedt, the boy who serendipitously stayed at home the day the bus stalled, was invited along. The children's primary physician at the Maxwell Hospital, Dr. Napoleon Burnett, traveled with them to attend to any physical needs that might arise. His eighteen-year-old daughter, Frances, attended as well. (Denver was not new to her. Her father served on the state board of health, and every month during his term the entire family traveled to the capital city.) Al Birch, *Post* correspondent and promotions manager, traveled to Holly to meet the group. He escorted the party the entire week.

The Pleasant Hill survivors, dressed in new clothing, assembled on Sunday, April 12, 1931, at the Holly depot. Some were bandaged or on crutches. The *Post* had reserved a plush Pullman car exclusively for the Pleasant Hill youngsters and their families. Fruit, sweets, and magazines were available, but the young people were too sleepy to enjoy the special treats, as the car was not scheduled to pull out of the station until 11:46 p.m. The scenery of the plains was masked by the dark night. The *clackety-clack* and motion of the train kept Clara Smith awake. The train stopped in Colorado Springs for breakfast, and by 10:00 a.m. on Monday, April 13—only nineteen days after the bus had stalled—they were in the big city.

And so began their week of *Denver Post* sponsorship. Upon their arrival at Denver's Union Station, a fleet of fancy new Buicks, courtesy of the Denver Buick Company, transported the guests up Seventeenth Street to the lavish Brown Palace, where they would stay. Rosemary Brown and Blanche Stonebraker, both suffering from frostbitten feet, were greeted by redcaps with wheelchairs who wheeled them from the train to the waiting cars. The children and their families had just enough time to check in and deposit their luggage in their rooms (*Denver Post* photographers snapping pictures the whole time) before the automobiles took the children to the *Denver Post* building on Champa Street, where they waved from a balcony and offered obligatory hellos into a microphone. Denver had, after all, been invited to "Meet Bus Survivors" at 12:15 p.m. that Monday, and an enormous crowd of curious spectators gathered on the street. Soft bedroom slippers protected the sore feet of most of the children. Rosemary Brown thought that these strangers regarded Pleasant Hill's children—waving from Fred Bonfils's balcony—as "remnants" or "leftovers" of a disaster. The whole week, she disliked the attention.

Rosemary relied on crutches to get around. Blanche Stonebraker could stand only long enough to pose for group photographs. She had to be carried everywhere, and sometimes her pain reduced her to tears. One of the chauffeurs took a liking to Blanche; after that, she was usually cradled in his sturdy arms.

On Monday afternoon, the visitors were driven to the gigantic Montgomery Ward store on South Broadway, where each of the six boys was given two new suits. Carl, Charley, and Max Huffaker, Leland Frost, and Bryan Untiedt chose long pants. Ome Untiedt chose one suit with long pants, and opted for knickers with the other. Each of the nine girls—Clara Smith, Eunice Frost, Rosemary and Maxine Brown, Alice, Lena, and Laura Huffaker, Evelyn Untiedt, and Blanche Stonebraker—received a silk dress. The J. C. Penney outlet in Holly had nothing like the immense selection of styles and colors in this big-city store! After their hour of shopping and fitting, each child was handed a balloon, and they embarked on a motor tour around Denver, passing Washington Park before returning to the Brown Palace. The offerings far surpassed any Christmas gifts they had ever received.

The two-room adobe and plank farmhouses of Pleasant Hill were far away now. Water need not be hauled into the house from the well outside this week; with a turn of the handle, water—even hot water—came right into the porcelain sink bowls in their rooms. There were no buckets of coal to carry and no stoves to stoke. Each family had its own room; large families were given two; and those rooms were bigger than the entire houses of Pleasant Hill with curtains made of material finer than flour sacks. Unseen chefs and helpers prepared sumptuous meals served on white china bearing the Brown Palace's initials with crystal water glasses and real silver tableware, all resting on linen (not oilcloth) tablecloths. The Pleasant Hill visitors' only duty was to sit at the banquet table in their new clothes. Outside the clean plate-glass windows sat shiny Cadillacs and Packards and Pierce Arrows.

Absent—but not forgotten—was a broken-windowed 1929 Chevrolet school bus trapped in a blizzard, where playmates muttered of being warm and then crumpled to the floor, dead.

❄❅❆❅❄

As Pleasant Hill's survivors took in Denver's sights, their friends from the west side returned to the school on the plains. Fourth-grader Wanda Crum and her west-end classmates felt the abject emptiness of the elementary schoolhouse. Some of their friends were in Denver exploring the town and getting gifts and staying in the Brown Palace— but some were dead. They would never return, and though Wanda and her classmates had personally seen their bodies in caskets two weeks earlier, the permanence was difficult to fathom. The seventh- and eighth-grade class had been depleted considerably; it now consisted only of Gerald Humrich and Helen Clapper. (Clara Smith was determined to finish out the year at the Pleasant Hill School, so she would return to the classroom when the Denver trip ended.)

Discontent simmered along the dusty roads of Pleasant Hill. Wanda Crum and her classmates knew that some parents were incensed at the teachers for turning the children out into the storm. Rumors circulated that someone might plant a bomb in the schoolhouse or lynch Maude Moser. She knew of the whisperings and appeared apprehensive every time a car pulled into the Pleasant Hill schoolyard. When an auto chugged down the seldom-traveled road past the school, Wanda stiffened, hoping the driver would not throw a bomb into their classroom. Most of the time the car merely carried curious outsiders who wanted to see the country school or its students who were struck by tragedy. No violence ever befell the Pleasant Hill School or its occupants, but the remaining students worried until the school year ended on May 22.

❋❊❋❊❋

Back in Denver, the survivors were treated like visiting royalty. On Monday, April 13, the Brown Palace hosted the initial banquet for the children and their families. Pink carnations adorned each place setting. Morgan O. Nichols, assistant manager of the Brown Palace, and F. W. Bonfils, business manager of *The Denver Post* and Fred Bonfils's nephew, welcomed the children to their weeklong home. Dinner entertainment was provided by a troupe of dancers the same age as the younger Pleasant Hill children. During dinner, leg pain attacked Blanche Stonebraker, and Alice Huffaker had to rely on others to wield silverware because her tender hands were swathed in bandages. Alice's mother took turns feeding her infant, Betty, and her fourteen-year-old, Alice. After filling themselves with grape-fruit, cream of tomato soup, chicken, potatoes au gratin, green peas, jockey club salad, and Neapolitan ice cream, the children proceeded in the waiting Buicks to the Rialto Theater to see the movie *Skippy*. Even the children in pain were thrilled with this lavish treatment.

Throughout the week the young people visited Denver's major attractions: City Park Zoo, where they were allowed to feed the animals; the Colorado Museum of Natural History; and the grave of "Buffalo Bill" Cody on Lookout Mountain. They feasted at the most expensive hotels and restaurants in town. One lunch took place at the Margery Reed Mayo Women's Club Social Center and Day Nursery, a particular interest of Fred Bonfils's daughter Helen. Rosemary Brown tasted homogenized milk for the first time and tried to keep a composed face at the awful taste. The evening entertainment ranged from a minstrel show in the City Auditorium, where the children had box seats, to movies at the Tabor Theater. They had their portraits taken at a professional photography studio, visited Governor Billy Adams in his office and observed sessions of the state Senate and House of Representatives, toured Denver on a private tramway car, and shopped for books and leather shoes. (It would be three months before the frozen feet of Blanche Stonebraker and Rosemary Brown would be able to fit into shoes.) Ome Untiedt's favorite part of the trip was the visit to the Fort Logan military installation near Englewood to observe a special exhibition drill and Army maneuvers. Ome would save the commemorative folder for years. About two thousand Denverites drove to see the drill and the Pleasant Hill people—"a double attraction," as the *Post* billed it.

The most memorable breakfast took place on Wednesday in the Oriental dining room of McVittie's Restaurant, 431 Seventeenth Street, hosted by ten-year-old June McVittie. Each Pleasant Hill youngster received a wristwatch, tidily wrapped and placed next to each dinner plate. Laura Huffaker was thrilled to get a real watch, her first one. Fully seventy-five of June's Park Hill Elementary School classmates attended the breakfast as well. Framed menus, headlined "A Colorado Morning Feast for Denver's Honored Guests," named a food delicacy after each survivor.

Parents accompanied their children to each banquet, performance, shopping expedition, and tourist site. Some were so humble that they found it difficult to accept the profusion of gifts, but they proceeded with the hope that the city excitements would erase some of the children's horrors. Other parents, having lost children in the tragedy, simply appreciated being in new surroundings where they were relieved of their everyday chores and responsibilities. Overall, the children sincerely enjoyed the activities, and to some extent the distraction worked. During the day, at least, the new experiences blocked their painful memories. At night, however, the bus reappeared in nightmares.

Eunice Frost's leg swelled suddenly, causing her excruciating pain. Dr. Burnett, always on call during the trip, examined the leg but could not relieve the swelling. It eventually went away, although the ache remained. The ever-present *Denver Post* photographers and reporters treated the children with respect. Nonetheless, being followed and lined up to pose for photos was an odd sensation that some children minded and others did not. Laura Huffaker never wore a hat at home, but found one on her head for photograph sessions.

Fred Bonfils wielded such influence in Colorado that a simple suggestion was all it took to recruit an advertiser or civic crony to help entertain the visiting families. In turn, participating businesses received free advertising and the assurance that they were involved in a worthy cause. This was the case even beyond major contributors such as the Denver Buick Company or the Brown Palace. "The gasoline tank of each car [transporting the children about town] was full of green Far-Go gasoline furnished by the Union Refining Company," was an example of the many endorsements the *Post* worked into newspaper stories of the youngsters' adventures. Bryan Untiedt's new wardrobe, which he would soon need when visiting the White House, was courtesy of the George F. Cottrell Clothing Company and the Oregon City Woolen Mills store. For the cost of a few items of clothing or a case of chocolates or chauffeur salaries, Denver entrepreneurs shared in the benevolent glow Bonfils exuded from his paper. In the Denver of the 1930s, business enterprises could be ensured prosperity by heeding the wishes of Fred Bonfils and his *Denver Post*.

Thursday afternoon the bus survivors toured the *Denver Post* building, and each young person was presented with an envelope containing an unspecified amount of cash, plus a gold-plated "heroism" medal enclosed in a purple-velvet-lined box, inscribed on the front: "Awarded by *The Denver Post* to [name]. April 16, 1931." A medal was set aside for widow Geneva Miller, who was still in Oklahoma visiting her parents. From the *Post*'s perspective, this event called for a news story, which stated in part that the presentation was among the "proudest moments of their lives," continuing:

> Since that tragic morning of March 26 when the school bus in which the children were riding was stalled by the storm, the entire nation has been heaping words and gifts of honor on the children. Yet it has remained for Mr. Bonfils to be the first to commemorate in immortal gold their heroic battle with the elements.

The accompanying story quoted Fred Bonfils: "Children, I love every one of you, but that is not why you are receiving these medals today. These medals are given you because of what you did out there when your school bus stalled in the storm, the way you sacrificed your own comfort and safety for that of your playmates."

Laura Huffaker proudly wore her medal during the remainder of her time in Denver. Eunice Frost felt that they were all heroes simply because they survived. Rosemary Brown disliked the term "hero," believing the children were victims of circumstances over which they had no control. The survivors later scarcely deemed the medal ceremony as their "proudest moment," but even as adults they sincerely treasured the medals.

Someone was inspired to arrange a "date" for Charley Huffaker during a party at Union Station during the week. Ten-year-old Darleen Hixson, song-and-dance performer during the evening, appeared to take an interest in thirteen-year-old Charley. The *Post* (A new angle! Romance!) deemed it page one news under the credit line of "By Charley Huffaker." "Charley Huffaker Loses Heart to Pretty Young Denver Singer," ran the headline. In fact, Darleen and Charley had been thrown together, and the story "By Charley Huffaker" was heavily embellished, based on a brief interview with him. Decades later he would laugh about the silliness of the contrived romance, but at the time Charley did not mind the attention. He took Darleen Hixson's address home and even wrote her once, but they never saw each other again. She remained, however, in his scrapbook of newspaper clippings.

The Lakeside Amusement Park was closed to other guests for two hours while the bus survivors rode the merry-go-round, miniature train, and roller coaster—the latter terrifying Alice Huffaker. Because of her bandaged hands she could not hold onto the car and was frightened of being flung out. Such incidents were not included in *The Denver Post* reports of the week's activities.

The children and their families constantly moved from one excitement to the next, some enjoying themselves and others uncomfortable with being on display. Clara Smith and Rosemary

Brown disliked the constant presence of reporters and photographers, and the curious stares of spectators. Eunice Frost, however, relished the new experiences and was not troubled by the staring eyes, and Maxine Brown felt like a princess. Charley Huffaker welcomed the distractions: Between the zoo, the amusement park, and the endless food, he found little time to dwell on the memories of thirty-three hours of torture. It was one of the most fun weeks he had spent in his twelve years. Bryan Untiedt took home a brand-new bicycle—nobody in Pleasant Hill had bicycles—and Clara Smith got a permanent wave and twenty-five dollars from the Victor, Colorado, Elks Lodge No. 367 in recognition of her "heroism."

The daytime return from Denver to Holly on Sunday, April 19, 1931, afforded the Pleasant Hill families a view of the scenery they had missed by riding the night train a week earlier. They saw springtime buds forming on the occasional trees, and the dry straw-colored buffalo grass of winter turning green.

Denver Post writer Al Birch, who had accompanied the visitors on their trek around Denver, escorted them home on the special *Post*-chartered Pullman car. They arrived in Holly, wearily, to yet another crowd—of an estimated three thousand spectators from southeastern Colorado and western Kansas. From the throng, a photographer shot moving pictures of them disembarking. The children of Pleasant Hill, who had survived a fatal blizzard, a whirlwind tour of the big city, and an avalanche of worldwide publicity, now endured an hour of filming before escaping in automobiles and being taken home, finally, to their dugouts and adobe houses.

Crammed in the back seat of a stranger's car with her mother and sister, Maxine, Rosemary Brown examined her gold medal. "Heroism," the inscription read. "Awarded by *The Denver Post* to Rosemary Brown. April 16, 1931."

Heroes they call us, she thought. *But we were just there, and couldn't get out.*

CHAPTER ELEVEN

A Political Pawn
from the Plains

BRYAN UNTIEDT, ONLY ELEVEN DAYS after returning from Denver, was off on his weeklong trip to Washington, D.C., at the invitation of President Herbert Hoover. *The Denver Post* managing editor, Edward Day, had suggested that the oldest girl from the Pleasant Hill bus, Clara Smith, also go to Washington, but the Hoover administration did not respond to that idea. Meeting and lunching with the president on April 30, Bryan met King Prajadhipok and Queen Rambai Barni of Siam, who were in the capital for an official state visit; toured the White House kennels; and observed the Supreme Court in session. He viewed the city from atop the Washington Monument; visited Ford's Theatre; dined with Herbert Hoover, Jr.; and received a gun as a gift from the president's other son, Allan. Bryan also was accompanied around the city by First Lady Lou Henry Hoover.

President Hoover's invitation to the young "hero" from Colorado had not been so altruistic as it appeared. Hoover, mired in the Great Depression—which he was unable to understand, let alone remedy—needed to improve his image as an aloof, dull man who largely refused to play the game of politics. (As he told an adviser prior to his campaign, "I'll kiss no babies.") Many Americans viewed him as a heartless, inhumane man who had thwarted legislation to relieve unemployment and had refused other measures that might have lessened the Depression's effects. Stung by criticism of their leader, Hoover's staff—particularly his press secretary, Theodore Joslin—searched for ways to humanize the commander in chief. The week of Bryan's visit, Hoover also hosted a group of anti-Prohibition women from both political parties, and his well-publicized new daily schedule included rising early to exercise and enjoying an afternoon "at the ballpark!" Having his picture taken with the famed farm lad from faraway Colorado fit neatly into the plan devised by Hoover's publicity strategists.

But Hoover's idea to draw upon Bryan Untiedt's hero image threatened to backfire. The Washington press corps wanted to interview Bryan, but the thirteen-year-old demurred because, as he divulged, he had promised *The Denver Post* an exclusive account of the journey. There was even suspicion that the *Post* was to pay Bryan

Bryan Untiedt on the White House lawn with President Herbert Hoover during Bryan's trip to Washington, D.C., from April 29 to May 2, 1931.

for the story. In fact, the account was to be written by Fred Warren, the reporter at the Reinert ranch who had likely proposed the idea of Bryan's heroism. Warren had planned to travel with Bryan to Washington, but under White House orders, Bryan was put on the train without Warren's knowledge, accompanied only by agent William H. Davenport of the US Secret Service office in Kansas City.

After the president's press secretary, Joslin, had arranged a meeting with a select group of reporters, Bryan informed the president that he could not be interviewed by the Washington correspondents because of his arrangement with *The Denver Post*. Greatly annoyed, the national reporters now decided to expose how the·*Post* was trying to exploit Hoover the way it had exploited Bryan Untiedt and the other survivors. Paul R. Mallon, president of the White House Correspondents Association, suggested that by hosting Bryan, "the White House was lending itself to a commercial venture." Joslin indignantly denied further accusations of participating in Bryan's "exploitation." At least, said former newspaperman Joslin, the White House had not been a conscious party to such a matter.

The president, in fact, tried to protect Bryan from excessive public exposure. When New York City radio personality Floyd Gibbons had earlier telegraphed Hoover asking for permission to bring Bryan to Manhattan for a weekend interview, the president refused, citing his concern for Bryan's "modest and retiring" demeanor and his own pledge to Bryan's parents to shield the boy from "unnecessary contact with strangers." Indeed, Hoover allowed only one brief photo session during Bryan's stay—that on the White House lawn.

A United Press Association report noted that Bryan, southeastern Colorado's "favorite son," had turned down offers including a New York movie company's trip around the world and vaudeville contracts of $1,000 per week. Hazel Untiedt, Bryan's mother, was reported as saying, "We do not want him to live on the honor of the nation. We want him to be a real man thru [*sic*] his own efforts and thus be entirely worthy of the honor President Hoover has bestowed upon him."

Bryan left Washington by rail on May 3, stopping in Chicago and arriving in Colorado May 5. *The Denver Post* related details of Bryan's trip to Washington, then featured an extensive photo-essay of the boy's farm life. Bryan's fellow survivors did not speak publicly about their thoughts on Bryan's trip. Privately, Charley Huffaker felt mildly jealous of Bryan's opportunity for such a visit, but he also felt sorry for Bryan having to shoulder the intrusive publicity. Maxine Brown, noting Bryan's new reluctance to look her in the eye, suspected that Bryan was ashamed to have accepted the accolades for actions he did not perform.

Some parents resented Bryan's favored press treatment and his extra gifts; it seemed unfair to them that he received more than their children did. The youngsters and their parents envied, for example, the new bicycle Bryan brought home from Denver. So great was Bryan Untiedt's fame that when he wrecked the bicycle, it became a national news story. Bryan also was offered a full scholarship, contingent upon his graduation from high school, to Washington College in Maryland. Bryan never accepted the offer.

Pleasant Hill families believed that some published accounts of Bryan's heroism were exaggerated. In one instance, Bryan's fame was utilized as social propaganda: The *Chicago Evening American* placed Bryan's photo next to that of a young murderer with the headline "Hero or Criminal? Which Will Your Child Be?" The article was reprinted in *The Denver Post* and other newspapers.

Bryan and the rest of the older survivors were invited to visit Pueblo for two days, May 13 and 14. There the young people—except Clara Smith, the only east-side student returning to finish the final three weeks of school following the Denver trip—watched their first semiprofessional baseball game and toured the Knuckles Meat Packing Plant, where they sampled fresh hot dogs. Later in the summer they traveled to Palmer Lake, the resort community northwest of Colorado Springs.

Back at the Pleasant Hill School, Clara joined Franz Freiday's remaining students from the west side, Helen Clapper and Gerald Humrich. Though Charley Huffaker and Bryan Untiedt did not finish the school year, they received their eighth-grade diplomas, which qualified them to proceed to high school. For reasons undetermined, the other eighth graders later had to pass the county test to attend high school.

The summer of 1931 continued painfully for all survivors, in one way or another. Alice Huffaker's hands cracked and itched for months while dead skin peeled off, and not until autumn did she regain their full use. Eunice Frost developed strep throat and a sty, both of which the doctor (perhaps erroneously) attributed to her time in the freezing bus. Blanche Stonebraker, who still could not stand, spent the summer crawling about the kitchen floor, using a chair as a counter upon which to help her mother prepare food. Her parents did not share with Blanche their grief of losing Louise, but their pain came out in other ways: Nellie Stonebraker, for example, invariably sang while working. Not that summer. Bud Untiedt developed insomnia, struck nightly with recurring visions of the dead and nearly dead children he found in their school bus.

After the tragedy, the children received mail addressed to them collectively and individually; written by strangers across the nation and even some from Europe and other faraway lands. Eunice Frost got a series of letters from a young man in the San Francisco area. He included a photo of himself, and she was intrigued enough to respond. He told her about a recent earthquake and mentioned that he would like to visit her someday. The postmarks, however, indicated to Eunice's father that the letters originated from Alcatraz, and soon the correspondence ceased. Eunice had found it rather exciting to have a pen pal.

Workmen set the monument in place as curious onlookers vie for a better vantage point. The monument for those lost and injured in the Pleasant Hill school bus tragedy was dedicated in 1931 at the Holly Cemetery. The man with white shirt and wooden tripod is a newsreel photographer. The two little girls in white skirts at right are thought to have been Pleasant Hill classmates.

Wanda Crum, who had been on the west-side bus, stood outside her farm home on a summer afternoon watching dust rise in the wake of an approaching auto. When it turned into her lane, the ten-year-old girl ran to fetch her father. A man carrying a notepad emerged from the car, asking a few brief questions about the Pleasant Hill bus. Wanda heard her father tell the man (Wanda never learned whether he was a reporter or an investigator) that he was certainly glad that none of his children rode the ill-fated bus. Also, a man with a briefcase showed up at the Frost household once or twice, speaking more with Eunice's parents than with Eunice or Leland, but the children never learned their topic of conversation.

That autumn, the younger Pleasant Hill children returned to classes, but rode a different bus. The older students—Clara Smith, Bryan Untiedt, Charley and Alice Huffaker, Eunice Frost, and Rosemary Brown—moved on to high school in Holly, since the Pleasant

Hill district did not have a high school. Bryan and Charley shared a boarding room that year, as did Alice and Eunice. Charley thought it odd that Bryan never talked to him about the bus or the following events. The Brown family had moved temporarily to Holly, so Rosemary and Maxine were able to reside at their new home in town.

The rural communities certainly had not forgotten the tragedy. On October 7, a ceremony at the Holly Cemetery dedicated a monument to the victims. Nearly seven hundred people attended—the Pleasant Hill School was among those canceling classes for the occasion—to hear an address by Irving P. Johnson, the Episcopal bishop of Colorado and member of the state board of corrections. "Out of suffering, great values come to men," he advised the crowd. "Human characters are developed. Suffering produces courage, generosity, resourcefulness, and persistence which combined is a nation's hope." One of the clergy who had officiated at the funeral, the Reverend I. J. Gorby, recapitulated the events of the previous spring, and then the Holly High School band played. Colorado lodges of the Independent Order of Odd Fellows, which had raised the funds for the monument, organized the dedication. After the carved stone slab was unveiled, children placed flowers on the graves. A time capsule containing press clippings was sealed inside the monument.

Whether in Holly or in the Pleasant Hill vastness, the children did not speak among each other of their thirty-three hours of hell. And when winter came and snows began falling, they inwardly cringed.

CHAPTER TWELVE

Later

IN MARCH 1932, parents Elmer and Margaret Brown, Reuben and Bessie Huffaker, and Bill and Ora Smith brought suit in the District Court of Kiowa County against the United States Fidelity & Guaranty Company, the Pleasant Hill school district's insurer. They argued that Carl Miller's bus was not properly equipped to withstand a storm and that the insurance company had been negligent by not examining the equipment it was insuring. The policy limited the liability of the company to $5,000 for a single personal damage and to $40,000 total damages. Legal proceedings did not conclude until September 1933—nearly two and a half years after the tragedy. Eventually, the insurance company settled in the probate court of Greeley County, Kansas—where the Huffakers and Browns resided at the time of the tragedy—awarding $900 to the Browns for Bobbie's death, $250 each for Rosemary's and Maxine's injuries, and $250 for each of the six Huffaker children who rode the bus. Clara Smith's family received $197.50 for her suffering. The varying settlements suggest that each family negotiated separately with attorney James M. Taylor, who represented the Denver branch of the Baltimore-based agency. The Brown and Huffaker children were never informed of the suit or settlements. The *Greeley County Republican* appears to have been the only newspaper reporting the legal actions and negotiated outcomes.

The Pleasant Hill bus tragedy inaugurated a decade of dramatic events and spirit-crushing circumstances for southeastern Colorado residents. Throughout the 1930s, droughts shriveled the already dry farmlands. What crops managed to sprout, legions of grasshoppers devoured. Dryland farming, already a challenge, became nearly impossible, and as crop yields dropped, prices rose. Across the plains, wind tore up the dry topsoil, whipping it into sudden and opaque dust storms. Hunger proliferated. With the 1933 advent of President Franklin Delano Roosevelt's national work-aid programs, unemployed fathers and older brothers were able to earn cash to support their families, but coin jars nationwide remained low. Hard work was not enough, and luck was in short supply.

Pleasant Hill's survivors relived their claustrophobia every time the stifling, blinding dust storms swirled around their farmhouses. A sudden onslaught of scarlet fever killed two young playmates of the Pleasant Hill children who had watched their siblings and friends freeze to death. Life in Kiowa County and its Pleasant Hill community trudged onward. Maude Moser moved away as soon as the 1930–1931 school year ended. She and her husband settled in Pueblo, where Moser taught fifth and sixth grades in the Vineland school district for the remainder of her career. She died in 1980. One of her two sons, John, related in 1999 that his mother always regretted her decision to send the children away in the school bus. She took her family to the site of the stalled school bus whenever they passed through southeastern Colorado.

Franz Freiday also left Pleasant Hill when the school year ended, relocating for the following two school years to the Pines, some ten miles west of Agate and a hundred miles northwest of Pleasant Hill. In 1932 he married Imo Coonts, who also taught at the Pines, and in 1934 the couple had a stillborn daughter. Scarcely four months after that, Freiday suddenly fell ill from a lung ailment and on October 27, 1934, he died at age twenty-seven at Colorado General Hospital in Denver. He is buried in Brighton's Elmwood Cemetery. Family members recall Freiday as being an able teacher who, in the few short years before his death, expressed great regrets over the Pleasant Hill tragedy and often talked of his responsibility in the matter. "It bothered him a lot," a family member recalls today. Imo Coonts Friday remarried, bore three sons, and remained a resident of eastern Colorado until her death in April 1985.

BLANCHE STONEBRAKER continued attending the Pleasant Hill School, though schoolwork presented a challenge for her. She and her parents talked freely about the bus tragedy. She related in 1999 that those uninhibited dialogues aided her emotional recovery. The loss of her older sister, Louise, affected Blanche less than it did her parents; in fact, Blanche remembers virtually nothing about Louise, the first to die in the Pleasant Hill bus. Blanche's single surviving memory of Louise involves an incident occurring some two years prior to the tragedy: The two little girls threw a ball back and forth on their father's new tractor.

Blanche Stonebraker Widger; Pueblo, Colorado: July 1998.

Blanche attended the first semester of ninth grade at Holly High School in 1938. She then resided with her grandparents in Severy, Kansas, to attend high school there, but at the end of the 1938–1939 school year she quit and returned home to her parents' farm in Pleasant Hill. Having given up on school, she moved to Eads to live in the National Youth Administration dormitory and sew uniforms for US troops during World War II. While there in 1941, a friend introduced her to butcher Donald Widger, who was working in a local grocery store. Six weeks after they met, they were wed. In 1943 while residing in a rented house in Eads, her son David Floyd Widger was born. One month premature, David was not expected to survive, but he did. Husband Donald continued to follow the lure of better-paying jobs, though once it meant spending three years working in Eads on the railroad. In 1945 the couple's second son, Richard Leroy Widger, was born. While he was still a baby, the Widgers moved from Eads to Syracuse, Kansas, where they remained for some twenty years. In 1946 Blanche gave birth to Donna Marie Widger. In 1952 the family spent a year in Holly living with Blanche's mother while Donald worked at Pugh Grocery.

In 1953 the Widgers moved to their first city, Pueblo, settling into an apartment near the Vineland district. When Blanche registered her children for school, she discovered that Maude Moser would be David's sixth-grade teacher. Blanche urged her husband to find another school district for them to live in, because she refused to let Moser teach her son.

When her children got older, Blanche spent seven years working as a cook at the Colorado State Hospital in Pueblo. In 1971 Blanche and Donald moved to Boulder. She cooked at Boulder Community Hospital from 1973 to 1978 while he continued to work as a butcher. After nine years in Boulder, the Widgers retired to Pueblo.

Donald Widger died in 1993, three weeks before the couple's fifty-second wedding anniversary. He told Blanche he had always felt honored to be married to a survivor of the famed bus tragedy. Blanche talked freely about the tragedy with him and their children from the time they were old enough to understand. "It was never a secret in our house. It's just something that happened and couldn't be helped," she relates.

Throughout the years Blanche Stonebraker Widger has remained in loose contact with Rosemary and Maxine Brown, Eunice Frost, and the Huffakers, and has remained very close to Wanda Crum. Blanche periodically discusses the bus tragedy with friends. Whenever the weather is cold and snowy, frightening memories rush to her. She remains continually astounded at the recollection of how close to death all the children were when her father and Bud Untiedt found the bus. Every Memorial Day Blanche visits the bus site and her father's grave in the Holly Cemetery. Rosemary Brown has informed Blanche that if ever Blanche is unable to make the trip, Rosemary will decorate Dave Stonebraker's grave because, as Rosemary states, "He saved my life." Still residing in Pueblo, Blanche has eleven grandchildren and nineteen great-grandchildren.

EUNICE FROST roomed with her cousin Alice Huffaker in Holly during their first year at Holly High School. The second year she roomed with Rosemary Brown. Eunice's parents were able to pay her room and board costs, so Eunice did not work in town. After her graduation in 1934, she resided with a family in Holly, caring for their children and performing housework.

Eunice Frost Youkey; McCook, Nebraska: July 1998.

Before the bus tragedy Eunice and her schoolmate Helen Clapper, who lived six miles west of the Frost farm, spent weekends at each other's homes. At Helen's home she met Helen's older brother, Joe. Eunice and Joe wed in 1936. During their first year of marriage they lived with his mother while Joe farmed the family property.

Farming was not Joe's calling, so he took a correspondence course and became a minister with the Assembly of God church. Thus began the Clappers' itinerant life of evangelizing around Colorado, California, and Nebraska. The five Clapper children were born during these years: Shirley Jo in 1937, Janice Marie in 1942, Claude Willard in 1945, Duane Douglas "Doug" in 1948, and Dwight Lee in 1951. When Dwight was a toddler, Eunice started working as a waitress, hostess, and cashier at restaurants in Schuyler, Nebraska, and in Omaha. In 1963 she became a cosmetologist and operated a beauty shop in Omaha and later in Beatrice, Nebraska. In 1972 the Clappers purchased a hotel in McCook, Nebraska, which they operated until 1979.

The most memorable parish Joe Clapper pastored originated in 1938 on the site of the stalled Pleasant Hill bus. Eunice recalls that "there were about nine members of that congregation who became ministers, so I believe it had a purpose to be built there." The church had been moved fourteen miles north from Pleasant Hill to Towner by the time he served there in the 1940s (it stood in 2000 as a private home), but it still held meaning for Eunice. After it had relocated, Eunice rarely visited the site of the stalled bus because she preferred not to trigger her memories of those thirty-three frightful hours. Joe died in 1981. Eunice worked as a waitress and remained in McCook, marrying retired horse trainer Norman Youkey in November 1983.

Widowed and residing in Columbus, Nebraska, Eunice has twelve grandchildren and fifteen great-grandchildren. She remains close friends with Rosemary Brown Cannon and communicates frequently with her cousins, the Huffakers. The bus tragedy remains an unpleasant topic, but Eunice's deep religious faith allows her to feel that "the Lord must have had some reason for it all."

LELAND FROST was seven years younger than his sister Eunice. Because of difficult times following the Dust Bowl, Claude and Mary Muriel Frost lost their farm and relocated to Towner. Claude found a job working as a janitor at Towner High School, which Leland attended until he graduated in 1941. Leland was drafted into the Army in June 1943, attended basic training at Camp Roberts in California, and a year later was sent overseas with other infantry regiments. Four months after arriving in Europe, his parents received a letter informing them that Leland "died in a European area from wounds received in action October 5, 1944." They never knew precisely where he was killed. Leland Frost was twenty years old—the only survivor of the Pleasant Hill tragedy to die young. Eunice and

Leland had never discussed the bus tragedy because of their age difference and different places of residence. Eunice believed that they did not know each other well enough to be comfortable discussing the school bus tragedy during the rare occasions in which they saw each other.

CLARA SMITH attended Pueblo Business College after graduating from high school in 1934, and in 1936 married Leland Speer, who also grew up in the Pleasant Hill–Holly community and had been among the rescuers. They lived in Westcliffe briefly, then moved to Wiley to farm. She suffered three miscarriages, and her doctor (probably mistakenly) attributed her childbearing difficulties to the hours on the bus. Nonetheless, the Speers were blessed with their first son, Darell, born in 1942. Clarence was born in 1945, and Gale in 1953. In 1963 the family moved to Fort Collins, where Clara was a cafeteria worker at the Woodward Governor Company and Leland contracted to do carpentry and plumbing work. As the eldest on the bus, Clara felt that she and Bryan Untiedt never deserved to be called heroes because the older children were obligated to share the responsibility of caring for the younger. She felt sorry that Bryan was burdened with the press attention and sensed Bryan's discomfort with the hero status. Clara spoke freely about the incident with her family, primarily with her husband and eldest son, Darell, but felt uncomfortable discussing it with people outside the family. In 1956 the television show "Once a Hero" approached her to appear regarding her experience on the Pleasant Hill bus. Though her family would have welcomed the remuneration, Clara refused. *Reader's Digest* later asked her to tell her story, but she declined that opportunity as well. Clara felt strongly that since every victim remembered the tragedy slightly differently, it would have been unfair for her to become the spokesperson. She also believed that the survivors had already been overexploited by the press. A stroke in 1991 robbed

Clara of clarity of speech, but not of the powerful memories of her frightening hours spent in the freezing bus. She died in 1997—on her wedding anniversary. Surviving her are three sons, four grandchildren, and five great-grandchildren.

CHARLEY HUFFAKER lived and worked in three different Holly homes during his years at Holly High School, performing whatever tasks the families needed—milking cows, fixing tools, and cleaning. Charley graduated from Holly High School in 1937—the year the rest of his family moved to Grove, Oklahoma—at which time he moved to Chazy, New York, to work briefly on a ranch. He then returned to his parents' home in Grove and worked

Charley Huffacker; Amarillo, Texas: June 1998.

on their farm until 1941 when he was drafted into the Army. He was stationed in Alaska from January 1942 until the end of the war. His sisters Lena and Laura graduated in 1941 from Grove High School with their friend Darlene Pigg. Darlene and Charley were married in Mississippi in 1944. He spent his career doing maintenance and carpentry work at the Veterans Administration Hospital at Amarillo, Texas. Daughter Linda was born in 1945, Gary in 1948, and Donna in 1950; they now have eight grandchildren and two great-grandchildren. They reside in Amarillo, Texas.

ALICE HUFFAKER suffered such badly frozen hands that nearly a year passed before the skin stopped cracking and peeling. After that, however, Alice's hands regained total mobility; in high school she even won a typing award. Alice attended Holly High School until her graduation in 1934. She and Eunice Frost shared a room in a private home in Holly for a year, and then Alice worked in a hotel for her room and board. She earned a dollar per week plus the tips she received for waiting tables. Eventually, she was hired as the cook, and her salary jumped to five dollars per week. She gave some of that money to her parents, saving the rest for a $30 sealskin coat.

In 1937 Alice accompanied the family to its new farm in Grove, Oklahoma. There Alice met Edgar Huggins, and they married in 1941. On a corner of their forty-three-acre

Alice Huffaker Huggins; Grove, Oklahoma: June 1998.

spread, the Hugginses ran a filling station/cafe/bake shop attached to a large building they rented out as a roller-skating rink and dance hall. Alice continued to work in the family store and in garment factories in Grove and nearby Miami after their three sons were born: Edgar Lee Roy in 1941; Charley in 1943; and Mickey in 1955. The skin on her hands continued to itch periodically until a relative furnished a salve of unknown ingredients that finally healed her hands.

After her husband died in 1967, Alice continued to run the filling station and to supervise garment factory workers. In 1968 she retired and sold parcels of land to neighbors. Alice lives on part of her remaining fifteen acres near Grove, brightening her property every summer with lush flower beds. She has five grandchildren and a great-granddaughter, some of whom live nearby. She and her siblings have stayed in close contact with the other survivors of the bus accident.

CARL HUFFAKER was the only Huffaker survivor who flatly refused to discuss his experience on the bus. Other traumatic experiences beset him during World War II service and at the Battle of the Bulge; he wanted to forget all the unpleasantness. Carl married Margie Wright in 1949. They lived in Claremore and Tulsa, Oklahoma, and briefly in Arkansas. Their first son died; three subsequent children survived: Richard was born in 1952, Billy Carl in 1954, and Patty in 1955. Carl Huffaker spent most of his career at Oklahoma Steel in Tulsa, then worked at McDonald's in later years. He died in 1981.

MAX HUFFAKER was drafted into the Army in 1942 and was wounded by shrapnel flung into his hip during World War II in Okinawa. Like Carl, he worked for Oklahoma Steel in Tulsa his entire adult life. He married Lorene Hunter in 1952 and became stepfather to her son, Wayne Hunter. He died in 1987.

LENA HUFFAKER graduated from Grove High School in 1941 with her younger sister Laura and their friend (and future sister-in-law) Darlene Pigg. She married Larry Nelson in 1945. Initially they lived in Enid, Oklahoma, where Larry was stationed in the Air Force. Their first child, Denny, was born in 1946, but right before Judy's birth in 1947, Larry left home. Lena returned to her parents' farm near Grove, Oklahoma, where her parents helped care for the children. Soon thereafter, her mother, Bessie, fell ill, and Lena became her caretaker until her death in 1971. Lena married H. L. Brock in 1975. Father Reuben Huffaker deeded the family farm to Lena, and she and H. L. lived there after the elder Huffaker's death in 1975. Lena died in February 1998.

LAURA HUFFAKER, the youngest of her family on the bus, moved to Grove, Oklahoma, with her family and spent her junior high and high school years there. She met Edgar Loehr in 1939, and they married in 1942. Five children followed: Archie in 1944, Liela in 1947, Alan in 1948, Peggy in 1951, and Shirley in 1955. Like Lena and Alice, Laura has been in the Grove area since 1937.

In the mid-1980s Laura Huffaker and her husband became trapped in their car during a sudden snowstorm. The third time they slid into the ditch, Laura says, "I just reached back and grabbed a blanket and told my husband, 'This is it,' and I just went out of it." She knew where she was and who was with her, but her mind blanked out sensation. When the storm was over and they were able to drive to a nearby cafe, she ordered an uncharacteristically huge breakfast and needed her husband's reassurance that it would be safe to use the restroom. This is the only occurrence she attributes directly

Laura Huffaker Loehr; Fairland, Oklahoma: June 1998.

to memories of the bus tragedy. Now living in Fairland, Oklahoma, the Loehrs have nine grandchildren and three great-grandchildren.

The Huffaker parents avoided the subject of the Pleasant Hill school bus because it was "such a sad time for everyone," Laura recalls. Her brother Charley believes that his parents preferred not to talk about it possibly because they were relieved—and perhaps felt some guilt—that all six of their children on the bus survived. Laura remembers Bess Huffaker, their mother, approaching the topic a few times about fifteen years after the bus tragedy, but at that time the survivors tried to avoid further discussions. Beginning with middle age, some of the Huffaker siblings brought up the bus topic occasionally during family gatherings. Only then did Max talk about the tragedy. Laura and Lena Huffaker seldom approached the subject. Lena discussed the death bus only when all the brothers and sisters were together. Charley rarely discussed the bus tragedy when he was young, and even then only with friends. His attitude was that there was no reason to dwell on unpleasant past events, especially when so many pleasant memories existed and so much life was yet to be experienced. In 1961 Charley returned to the bus site for the monument dedication ceremony, also attended by Rosemary Brown Cannon, Clara Smith Speer, Ome Untiedt, and Bryan Untiedt. His few visits to the site since then have been relatively unemotional, and he feels that the experience has affected him minimally throughout his life.

MAXINE BROWN continued attending the Pleasant Hill School until 1935 (except for the 1931–1932 year spent in Holly) when her parents moved to Sublette, Kansas. She entered high school there but returned to Holly to live with her sister, Rosemary, and Rosemary's husband, Jack Cannon. There she completed high school in 1940. Maxine then left Rosemary's fun-loving home (Maxine appreciated Jack because he was a prankster and loved to laugh) and joined her parents in Idaho. She recalls the year she spent there on their sandy, cold farm as the loneliest in her life.

Maxine escaped to Ogden, Utah, and entered beauty school. The eighteen-year-old rented an apartment above a mortuary and worked part-time wrapping cookies in a Wonder Bread bakery. She grew suddenly ill and had to return to her parents' home to be nursed back to health. Upon recovery, she moved back to Ogden, this time to work as a restaurant cashier, waitress, and manager. For the next five years Maxine shared an apartment with two other women and saved money. Because she was young and single, she liked moving around, going "wherever the light looked better."

In her early twenties Maxine moved to Lamar to work at a telephone company, then transferred to Portland, Oregon, and later worked in naval shipyards. In Portland she met her first husband, Steven Brossart, and they had four children: Steven Mark was born in 1951, Ray in 1953, Jack in 1954 (named after her brother-in-law, Jack Cannon), and finally Susan in 1959—the daughter she wanted so badly. That marriage soon ended. Maxine worked a variety of jobs throughout her life, taking time off only when her children were young. She lived in Portland until 1990 when she married "the love of my life," Verne Foreman, and moved to Silverton, Oregon.

Reflecting on her childhood, Maxine believes that though she was poorer in the 1930s than at any subsequent time in her life, she was also the happiest. She treasures her childhood friends and her sister; she remained especially close to Lena Huffaker, whose birthday was only three days after hers.

Maxine Brown Foreman (left) and Rosemary Brown Cannon; Holly, Colorado: May 1998.

Maxine's husband, Verne, was reared in Stratton, Colorado, and before their marriage he once casually inquired if she recalled a school bus that stalled in a ditch and children froze to death. She responded, "You're talking to a survivor—can you believe that?" She discussed the matter with him on that occasion but avoids further discussions or thoughts on the subject. Still residing in Oregon, she appreciates weather that does not remind her of Pleasant Hill. The Columbine High School massacre in April 1999 near Denver, however, elicited the same horror she had felt when her brother and classmates died tragically in the 1931 blizzard.

Maxine visits her sister, Rosemary, periodically, but barely recognizes their former neighborhood of farms. Now irrigation lines, fences, and new houses partition the land. She loves Oregon and plans to remain. All four children live in Portland, as do four grandchildren. She suffered a mild stroke in 1999.

ROSEMARY BROWN is the only survivor who has lived her entire life near the bus site. The Brown family moved from Pleasant Hill to Holly during the 1931–1932 school year so the elder Brown boys, Harold and Roy, could finish high school and Rosemary could begin. The boys never finished and moved back to the farm, but Rosemary remained in school. In 1932, she met Jack Cannon during a Holly High School musical production. After she graduated in 1935, they married and moved to nearby Syracuse, Kansas, where Jack operated a filling station. Their first child, Richard, was born in 1938 on March 26—the anniversary of the bus tragedy. Cheryl was born in 1943, and Jill in 1947.

Rosemary and Jack stayed in the Holly area. In the early 1950s, Rosemary spent three years working as a bookkeeper at Holly Lumber Company. Her husband knew that she had been aboard the bus because he lived in the community in 1931, but they rarely discussed her experiences. She did not tell her children of the bus until 1989; the subject was too painful to discuss. Even she and Maxine, who grew closer as they matured, only occasionally talked about their memories or feelings related to the bus incident. Rosemary's guilt over Bobbie's death never abated. In 2000, Rosemary still cherishes the *Denver Post* hero medal and appreciates the gifts and the lavish trip to Denver, although she agrees that "we were neither physically nor mentally prepared for all of that"; and feels that the *Post* "did use us for a sensational story."

When she wrote a brief history of her recollections for the Kiowa County Historical Society in 1989, she confronted the memories, and finally the nightmares lessened. Still, "it hurts to the bone," she attests. Rosemary now has eight grandchildren and seven great-grandchildren. Jack died in 1998. Rosemary is the only survivor still residing in Holly. "I've forgotten a lot," she says. "I wish I could forget more."

OME UNTIEDT attended high school in Holly, working at the local hotel for his room and board. He then moved to Denver, eventually starting a construction business. He rarely mentioned the bus incident that had caused his family so much pain and the loss of a child. His widow, Faye, believes that the publicity and the loss of Ome's brother Arlo troubled Ome his entire life. Ome died in 1981.

EVELYN UNTIEDT attended high school in Bartley, Nebraska. When her mother, Hazel, died in 1937, Evelyn returned to the farm near Holly to raise her siblings. Later she moved to Denver to be near her brothers Bryan and Ome, with whom she had always felt close. In Denver, she met and married Larry Chandler. Evelyn discussed the general topic of the bus more often than her brothers did, but she would not address specifics of the thirty-three hours on the bus. In 1989 she penned eight pages of her recollection for her children, Larry and Gary. In that brief memoir, she stated that the designation of hero and heroine for Bryan and Clara was "an honor they both deserved and earned." Regarding the trips to Denver and Pueblo, Evelyn felt that the fun and distraction they provided genuinely helped her to recover emotionally from the bus tragedy. She saved in her cedar chest the dress she wore during the blizzard, the dress she received in Denver, and a white beaded purse Bryan brought her from Washington, D.C. Evelyn died in 1990.

BRYAN UNTIEDT was denied the Carnegie Medal in November 1931, with no public explanation. This did not affect the general perception of him as a hero, however; the following March, Bryan toured the West Coast—under the auspices of socialite Mrs. Alexander Kerr—speaking at child welfare institutions. There, he met movie star Tom Mix, who gave him a medal for bravery, and rode one of Rudolph Valentino's Arabian horses.

Bryan left the family farm for Denver at age sixteen, after completing his sophomore year at Holly High School. He never graduated from high school or accepted the proffered scholarship to college, largely because his father, Bud, regarded higher education as a waste. Bryan worked for a week as a page in a special session of the Colorado Legislature in November 1936 before starting a steady job at a packing plant. The following year he joined the Colorado National Guard, and in 1942 he enlisted in the Navy. He started construction companies on his own and built hundreds of quality, affordable homes. Two of those he showed in the Parade of Homes, one of which was in his own development, Park East in Aurora.

Frances "Pinky" Wayne of *The Denver Post* wrote in 1931 that Coloradans "are going to watch you [the Pleasant Hill survivors] and your gallant leader, Bryan Untiedt, as you grow into manhood and womanhood." Her prediction was, unfortunately for Bryan, true. On anniversaries of the tragedy, reporters contacted Bryan for some sort of comment, but received firm (and often impolite) rebuffs. When he was out of work, or was once cited for public intoxication (at age eighteen), or received a traffic fine, his name hit the newspapers. The continuing and unwanted media attention deeply frustrated Bryan; he felt that because his every move was publicized, he had been robbed of the freedom to make mistakes.

Bryan's popular status as a child celebrity followed him throughout his life, despite his adamant refusals to discuss the bus tragedy. He answered reporters' questions only a few times and attended the 1962 monument dedication at the site of the stalled bus, but was loathe to bring up the subject of the tragedy even with his own family. The only comment he made to his wife of twenty-two years, Margery, was, "I just did what anybody would have done." His children never received satisfactory answers to their questions about the bus tragedy or, indeed, about any part of his difficult Depression childhood. When they queried their grandfather, Bud Untiedt, he only said, "Ask your father about it. It is his story to tell."

The family remembers Bryan relating drawn-out tales of his years in the construction industry. He was a "self-made man," as Margery points out, proud that he helped build Red Rocks Amphitheatre in the foothills west of Denver and homes in the city's burgeoning suburbs.

The myth of Bryan Untiedt's "heroism" followed him to his grave. At his death in December 1977, his family supplied obituary data, but newspapers again revived the old heroism reports. Family members long ago had dismissed the notion that Bryan had disrobed in the bus and given his garments to the smaller children—it would have meant death within minutes—but there it appeared again in the *Post* obituary. Nonetheless, in 1999 Bryan's daughter Teresa spoke for the family in the belief that "He was a hero to us." Bryan's additional survivors include daughters Judi, Linda, Samantha, and son Jon.

❋❋❋❋

In 1991, the eight remaining Pleasant Hill survivors reunited in Holly at Rosemary Brown Cannon's home. Most had kept in touch with each other, at least through letters. Rosemary and Maxine Brown, Clara Smith, Eunice Frost, and Alice, Lena, Charley, and Laura Huffaker shared memories of their childhoods on the farm, but talked little about the tragedy.

In 2000, Kiowa County Road 78 leading north out of Holly (to Towner) passes the cemetery before heading through miles of flat farmland. Kiowa County's estimated population is down to 1,716, with about 850 of those residing in Eads. Many fields lie fallow as a result of government-sponsored aid programs. Telephone poles and trees shading the intermittent houses or barns interrupt the smooth horizon. Few cars travel this road. Seventeen miles north of Holly, on the west side of the road, a polished stone slab marks the site of the 1931 bus tragedy. Engraved on it are the names of six people who died there.

Today's children ride radio-equipped, heated buses to Holly's big schoolhouse. Still, across these plains, nothing blocks the wind.

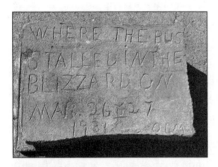

The small picture is of a hand-made commemorative concrete slab placed at the crash site shortly after the event. The larger photo shows that the original small slab was left in place when the tall granite monument was subsequently dedicated in 1962.

In 2024, three monuments commemorate the Pleasant Hill school bus calamity: the large monument alongside the gravestones at the Holly Cemetery; the monument at the crash site and shown here on page 140, and this four-sided diorama in Towner at the intersection of Colorado Highway 96 and the Holly-Towner Road, now designated as Kiowa County Road 78.

Notes

CHAPTER ONE
The Children of Pleasant Hill

1. The biographical data regarding Maude Moser comes primarily from her son, John L. Moser. Fern Reinert remembered residing in the same house with Maude Moser when Fern and her husband were newlyweds in 1926. This indicates that Moser lived at the Reinert home in the Pleasant Hill district for at least five years. The year 1931 marked Moser's first year teaching at the Pleasant Hill School, however. In 1930, the Pleasant Hill School was consolidated with another elementary school, New Hope, that stood adjacent to the Stonebraker property. The children on the east bus attended New Hope before the building itself was moved to the Pleasant Hill location. Moser may have taught at the original Pleasant Hill School that none of these "east bus" children attended, or she may have taught at a school in a neighboring district. Moser's son cannot recall her teaching history, and the county school records are not that specific.

2. There is no consensus regarding where Friday resided. Wanda Crum recalls that Friday and Moser both boarded at the August Reinert home, but Fern Reinert disagrees. *The Denver Post* mentions at one point that Friday boarded at the Albert Crum home, and Eunice Frost and Blanche Stonebraker remember that as well. *The Denver Post* later implies that Friday resided at the Charles Humrich home—the home of one of the west-side children.

3. Friday was hired to teach the older children when the Pleasant Hill district consolidated into a school with two buildings. Newspaper accounts referred to Franz Friday as the principal of Pleasant Hill School. According to the permanent teacher records and certification (file box 13021, Colorado State Archives, Denver), Freiday and Moser were paid the same salary and had the same responsibilities—there was

no evident hierarchy. Indeed, Moser had more teaching experience than Freiday. The children did not view Freiday as the principal, so the authors refer to him as a teacher.

4. Community members today recall the blame falling on Maude Moser as the person deciding to send the children away on the bus. However, Freiday was the spokesperson for the school district in subsequent newspaper interviews. The children who overheard the conversation between the teachers and the bus driver deduced that Carl Miller was reluctant to make the trip, but their memories remain vague about which teacher did more of the talking. Alice Huffaker overheard the conversation among the adults, but she does not remember exact words. Charley Huffaker assumed that because the teachers made their decision so quickly, "their minds were already made up by the time we got there." Without clear evidence that Moser talked both men into the decision to send the bus away, both teachers are presented here as the decision-makers.

CHAPTER TWO
Lost

5. On Sunday, March 29, after news of the tragedy had spread across the United States, curious people within driving distance traveled to the site of the stalled bus to learn as much as they could. That clear afternoon, the editor of the *Greeley County* [Kansas] *News* tried to retrace Carl Miller's confused wanderings across the fields to the fatal location. He wrote a complicated account of Miller's twistings and turnings that, without an accompanying map, was impossible to follow.

CHAPTER THREE
The First Day

6. Some remember the fire being built in a lunchpail, some remember it being a cream or gallon syrup can that was used as a lunchpail, and some remember it as the milk can used to haul water, which was fastened to the running board. A photograph subsequently taken of the bus interior suggests, however, that the fire was started in the milk can lid.

7. The order of events during this long imprisonment on the bus differs in the survivors' memories. After interviewing all survivors at length, the authors have established the most logical and consistent sequence to facilitate a smooth narrative.

8. Specifics of Franz Freiday's and Maude Moser's actions after the bus left the schoolhouses remain vague. *The Denver Post* reported that Freiday remained at the schoolhouse Thursday and Friday, and on Friday afternoon helped Oscar Reinert and Albert Crum carry coal to the Crum residence. Wanda Crum recalls two men delivering doughnuts and boiled eggs to the house and is positive that neither was Freiday. It is possible that Wanda could have been otherwise occupied at the time Freiday visited, if he did. He also could have left the school earlier and found shelter or made it home—wherever that was. Maude Moser found safety somewhere, but research has not divulged where.

9. Frequent urination is a component of hypothermia. Although the children had nothing to drink and do not recall even being thirsty, hormones and kidneys function in a very cold body by constricting blood vessels and increasing fluid output. This is why the children, especially the smaller, thinner ones who would have become colder sooner, probably wet their pants on a regular basis.

10. Survivors agree that Carl Miller may have said something to Bryan Untiedt and Charley Huffaker, since they were the oldest boys, about watching over the younger children. Evelyn Untiedt wrote in a 1989 recollection that Miller told Bryan to "keep all of them alive that you can," but none of the others remembers hearing such a remark being directed solely to Bryan. Clara Smith Speer later recalled Miller telling each of the older children (Bryan, Charley, Alice, Clara, Eunice, Rosemary, and Louise) to choose one younger person to look after. Maxine and Rosemary Brown felt that Miller's statement was a blanket order to the older children to take care of the younger ones. The sisters point out today that in the 1930s it was common for older children or adults to protect young children, regardless of familial relationships.

11. Most survivors recall Louise Stonebraker sitting on the bench, and nobody moving her after she died. Maxine Brown is the only one who remembers Louise sliding off the bench, landing on her knees, and her eyes turning "multicolored." Louise's younger sister, Blanche, recalls Kenneth Johnson's mother relating later that Louise was menstruating that day, which could explain why she didn't feel like exercising: either she was experiencing cramps or she was embarrassed to stand and expose her blood-stained dress.

CHAPTER FOUR
Waiting

12. It has not been learned when exactly Freiday returned to his boarding home, or where he boarded.

13. Survivors remember Kenneth Johnson dying abruptly. When human body temperature sinks to the low range of 82.4 to 86.0 degrees Fahrenheit, the heart muscle contracts spasmodically and irregularly, which can cause heart failure. This may have been what happened to Kenneth Johnson. Regarding the earlier fatalities, it is most likely that body temperatures lowered so much that the children exhibited signs of death (stiffness, undetectable heartbeat, unconsciousness) before the heart muscle actually stopped. The other children would not have known the precise point of death for this reason (according to Dr. Michael Yaron, associate professor of emergency medicine at the University of Colorado Health Sciences Center—see bibliography). Clara Smith Speer recalled carrying Kenneth Johnson to the back of the bus. Whether Kenneth Johnson or Bobbie Brown died first is not clear. Both, however, seem to have died within a short time of each other. Clara Smith Speer seemed more certain than the others that Bobbie died before Kenneth did.

CHAPTER FIVE
Blankets and Fried Potatoes

14. Most survivors and newspaper accounts mention Bud Untiedt and Dave Stonebraker as having located the bus. Some news reports indicate that Ernest Johnson, rather than Dave Stonebraker, was one of the two rescuers. Johnson undoubtedly was present at the Reinert ranch, which may be the source of some of the confusion. The survivors unanimously recall only two rescuers. Research has failed to divulge when or how Bud Untiedt met up with Dave Stonebraker. According to Geneva Miller, Stonebraker rode to the Ernie Johnson place. Johnson proceeded with Stonebraker on horseback to the Pleasant Hill School, carrying enough sandwiches for the twenty children. On the way, they stopped at Carl Miller's farm, where a candle still burned in the window. Geneva Miller anxiously reported that her husband had not returned from delivering the children, at which point Johnson and Stonebraker continued. According to stories Clara Smith Speer heard, however, Johnson set out with the sandwiches, found the school empty,

continued to the Crum house where he deposited the sandwiches, then went to the Untiedt place where he informed Bud Untiedt of the missing children. Then, Untiedt and Stonebraker set out in Stonebraker's wagon with food that Hazel Untiedt had prepared, while Johnson continued searching separately. Any of the above is reasonable; the authors have selected one version arbitrarily.

15. In Depression-era farm culture, people in trouble helped each other regardless of their relationship or level of familiarity. Most people in the Pleasant Hill community knew each other at least by sight, so it would not have been unusual to welcome strangers or acquaintances in need. The decision to take seventeen children to the nearest farmhouse was not only the sole option Untiedt and Stonebraker had at that point, but also the most expedient. Removing them to their own homes farther away would have further jeopardized the children's lives.

16. News reports erroneously referred to the Reinert house as "two-room." Fern Reinert explained that there were two main rooms—a kitchen and a bedroom—and two tiny bedrooms on the north side of the house. Most survivors recall being placed in the large room that served as kitchen and living area. John Kenneth Herrick, a ranch hand who was at the farmhouse all night, remembers the children lying on the floor of the main room.

17. The accepted method of frostbite treatment in the 1930s was to warm the skin slowly. Therefore, treatment included rubbing skin with snow and ice to prevent rapid rewarming. External application of distillate or diesel fuel was thought to achieve the same result—the cooling effect increasing circulation without allowing the skin surface to grow too warm. Scientists have since disproven this theory. Today's accepted method of treating frostbite is to immerse the affected area in warm water. Massaging, which the men at the Reinert ranch did all night on the children's frozen parts, was thought to increase blood flow to the skin, thus warming it. However, manipulating tissue that has already been damaged further destroys cells. A likely hypothesis is that because the children's limbs recovered fully, despite treatment so obviously detrimental to fragile tissue, the frostbite must have been fairly mild. The only solid conclusion reachable regarding the Pleasant Hill children, in the absence of their medical data, is that a wide variation of responses exists within the human body.

18. Fern Reinert told the authors that she and her husband did not store diesel fuel inside the house, as it was volatile. Some children do not remember diesel fuel being rubbed on their frozen body parts; Clara Smith Speer and Evelyn Untiedt remembered it, and John Kenneth Herrick recalls using it. Some newspaper reports mention it as well. If fuel were indeed used, a neighbor would have brought it. With regard to the whisky, ingesting alcohol promotes a sensation of warmth, but in reality, causes the blood vessels to dilate, making the skin feel warm but increasing the amount of surface area from which the heat can escape.

19. A person in severe stages of hypothermia can exhibit signs of being dead—cold, stiff, lifeless, and with a heartbeat so faint that it is virtually undetectable—yet still be saved. Even after Arlo Untiedt and Mary Louise Miller had probably been dead for hours, the men were still massaging them, hoping the signs of death were only signs. At what point Mary Louise and Arlo died is uncertain. Most survivors who recall the hours at the Reinert ranch estimate that they both expired before midnight; Evelyn Untiedt believes that Mary Louise died soon after their rescue. The death certificates, which only state an approximate time of death, do, however, list Friday, March 27 as the date of death. Clara Smith Speer thought Mary Louise may have died in the wagon on the way to the Reinert residence. Geneva Miller, however, was under the impression that when the neighbor men left the Reinert home to inform her about her missing husband and afflicted daughter, Mary Louise was still alive. Bud Untiedt told Ome's daughter Jo that when he reached the bus, Arlo did not seem to be in an alarming condition, so when the rescue party arrived at the Reinert farm, Untiedt vigorously rubbed the other children to keep them alive. Because Arlo was still talking coherently, Untiedt propped him in a corner and went to work on the other children: When Bud next looked, Arlo was dead. Rosemary Brown, however, recalls that even while on the bus the children were worried about Arlo and Mary Louise because they seemed to be failing. She recalls that Bud Untiedt paid special attention to Arlo because of Arlo's desperate state.

20. It has not been determined exactly how the news was circulated beyond the Reinert farm. It is most likely that the *Lamar Daily News* alerted the news wire services. Alternatively, *The Denver Post* could have received a telephone tip.

21. Whether both Kenneth and Bobbie were at the back of the bus is uncertain. The interior was quite small, so when the fathers opened the door

they would have seen the dead children easily no matter where the bodies were located. There is no record or recollection of the identities of those who removed the bodies, or proof of where the bodies were immediately taken. Maxine Brown recalls hearing that the bodies were taken to the Brown household, since Bobbie Brown was among the dead. Some believe the removal occurred late Friday night, though it would have been reasonable to have waited until daylight. The *Greeley County News* reported that shortly after Friday midnight, an "ambulance from Holly had just removed the five bodies."

22. Timing is difficult to determine because those present simply remember a long night filled with adults. The *Greeley County News* reported that Dr. Hubener and his caravan from Tribune reached Towner just after midnight and the Reinert farm a little after 1:00 a.m. Howard Huddleston, a resident of Towner in 1931, related to the curator of the Greeley County Museum in 1991 that the Tribune doctor and his twenty-three helpers rode the train from Tribune to Towner, then pushed autos through drifts to the ranch. This was never recorded, and Huddleston is not alive to query.

CHAPTER SIX
"Ship of Mercy"

23. Although Ome Untiedt's family told the authors that Bud Untiedt would not have encouraged the *Post* to make his son Bryan a hero, Clara Smith Speer remembered hearing the conversation, as quoted here, between the reporter and Untiedt. Blanche Stonebraker relates that her father told her many times that he also overheard this conversation. The *Post* newsmen were the first on the scene; it was common practice, particularly in the 1930s, for journalists to borrow "facts" from competing newspapers. Once the notion was circulated that Bryan was the hero, there was no stopping the story. On March 26, 1961, Vaughn Swafford wrote to *The Denver Post* that he had been a member of the rescue party, and that he also was "responsible for Bryan Untiedt getting the buildup he got, which resulted in President Hoover's inviting him to come to Washington." Whether this means that Swafford planted the idea in reporter Fred Warren's head that Saturday will never be determined.

24. One of the Romer sons, Roy, served as Colorado governor from 1987 through 1999.

25. Geneva Miller recalled in the early 1990s that her husband was not wearing his coat when his body was found. Her source of information is unknown. Accounts in *The Denver Post* and the *Lamar Daily News* mention that he was wearing his overcoat, whereas the *Rocky Mountain News* reported that his hat and overcoat were gone and his suit coat was unbuttoned. Most survivors remember Miller asking for his coat back from Bryan, but Alice Huffaker thinks Miller left the coat with Bryan and went into the cold without it. Reports vary widely, stating that from fifty to one thousand men searched for Miller's body. Leland Speer, who later married Clara Smith, was the second person to encounter Miller's body after Ralph Lucius found it. Clara Smith Speer's memoirs include her husband's vivid recollection of Miller's lacerated hands.

CHAPTER EIGHT
And a Hero Is Created

26. Charley Huffaker was close friends with Bryan Untiedt before and after the bus incident. Bryan and Charley never discussed the tragedy or its aftermath, even though the following year they roomed together in Holly. Today, Huffaker states firmly that he means no disrespect toward Bryan, but insists that Bryan did not perform any heroic actions.

27. Hearst Metrotone News was one of the companies that shot footage shown in brief clips at local movie theaters. Filmed interviews with Clara Smith and Bryan Untiedt on April 15, as well as coverage of Bryan visiting Washington, D.C., on May 2, were at one time housed in the University of California at Los Angeles (UCLA) Film and Television Archives, but the film has since been discarded. Film clips by Pathe News of Oklahoma also aged and were destroyed. The authors' aggressive search for any motion picture footage in other film archives has yielded no results thus far.

28. After Clara Smith's 1936 marriage to Leland Speer, a doctor in Lamar attributed her several miscarriages to her having been on the cold bus. Current medical theories do not support this.

CHAPTER NINE
Going Home

29. The puzzling suggestion here, that the teachers would pay part of Oscar Reinert's salary, cannot be presently explained.

Bibliography

Books and magazine articles

Coons, E. N. *36 Hours of Hell*. Muskogee, Okla: Hoffman Printing Company, 1988.

Fowler, Gene. *Timber Line: A Story of Bonfils and Tammen*. Garden City, N.Y.: Covici & Friede, 1933.

Greeley County Historical Book Committee. *History of Early Greeley County: A Story of Its Tracks, Trails, and Tribulations*. Tribune, Kan.: Greeley County Historical Book Committee, 1981.

Hart, Stephen S., and Thomas J. Noel. "You Got that Dust Pneumonie," *Colorado Heritage*, Autumn 1997.

Hosokawa, Bill. *Thunder in the Rockies: The Incredible* Denver Post. New York: William Morrow & Company, Inc., 1976.

Ingram, Tolbert R., comp. and ed. *Year Book of the State of Colorado*. Denver: State Board of Immigration, 1930 and 1932.

Leonard, Stephen J. *Trials and Triumphs: A Colorado Portrait of the Great Depression, With FSA Photographs*. Niwot, Colo.: University Press of Colorado, 1993.

Pearson, Georgene. *A Light in the Window*. Tulsa, Okla.: Logos to Rhema Publishing, 1995.

Pozos, Robert S., and David O. Born. *Hypothermia: Causes, Effects, Prevention*. Piscataway, N.J.: New Century Publishers, Inc., 1982.

Reish, Edward C., Virginia Downing, and Thomas Nidey. *Lamar, Colorado: Its First Hundred Years, 1886–1986*. Lamar, Colo.: Edward C. Reish, Virginia Downing, and Thomas Nidey, 1986.

Secrest, Clark. "How Colorado Blew into Kansas," *Colorado Heritage*, Winter 1994.

Teal, Roleta D., and Betty Lee Jacobs, comps. *Kiowa County*. Kiowa County, Colo.: Kiowa County Bicentennial Committee, 1976.

Manuscript collections

Aircraft log book, 1931, Folder 3022, Box 100, Humphreys Manuscript
    Collection 925, Colorado Historical Society, Denver.
County Superintendent Record Book, Vol. 5, 1930–1931, File of District
    No. 17, Box 13016, Colorado State Archives, Denver.
Education Management Services Teacher Experience Cards, 1928–1958,
    Roll 11, Colorado State Archives, Denver.
Education Superintendent of Schools Annual Reports, 1931, Kiowa County,
    Roll 34, Colorado State Archives, Denver.
Permanent Teacher Records, Kiowa County Superintendent Records, Box
    13021, Colorado State Archives, Denver.
Petition for appointment of guardian and guardian's bond for Clara Smith,
    probate court case number 533, Greeley County, Kan., September
    14, 1933, Greeley County Probate Court, Tribune, Kan.
Petition for appointment of guardian and guardian's bond for the minor
    Huffaker children, probate court case number 532, Greeley County,
    Kan., September 14, 1933, Greeley County Probate Court, Tribune,
    Kan.
Presidential papers, secretary file, Bryan Untiedt, Box 908, Herbert Hoover
    Presidential Library, West Branch, Iowa.
Superintendent Records, 1900–1969, Box 13021, Colorado State Archives,
    Denver.

Memoirs

Chandler, Evelyn Untiedt, January 1989. Personal collection of Untiedt
    family, Louisville, Colo.
Speer, Clara Smith, 1957–1970. Personal collection of Darell Speer, Fort
    Collins, Colo.
Youkey, Eunice Frost, 1950–1960. Personal collection of Eunice Frost
    Youkey, Columbus, Neb.

Interviews

Cannon, Rosemary Brown. With Ariana Harner. Holly, Colo., May 28,
    1998.
———. With Clark Secrest. Holly, Colo., October 1993.
———. With Vicki Hildner, producer, KCNC-TV, Denver. Holly, Colo.,
    December 1997.

Crum, Wanda. With Ariana Harner. Cañon City, Colo., July 11, 1998.

Foreman, Maxine Brown. With Ariana Harner. Holly, Colo., May 28, 1998.

Huffaker, Charley. With Ariana Harner. Amarillo, Tex., June 20, 1998.

Huggins, Alice Huffaker. With Ariana Harner. Grove, Okla., June 15, 1998.

Loehr, Laura Huffaker. With Ariana Harner. Fairland, Okla., June 16, 1998.

Moser, John. Telephone interviews with Ariana Harner. Pueblo, Colo.,
    August 11, 1998; September 8, 1998.

Pearson, Georgene. With Ariana Harner. Oologah, Okla., June 17, 1998.

Reinert, Fern Frost. With Ariana Harner. Eads, Colo., May 29, 1998.

Speer, Clara Smith. With Clark Secrest. Fort Collins, Colo., October 1993.

Speer, Darell. With Ariana Harner and Clark Secrest. Fort Collins, Colo.,
    March 10, 1999.

Untiedt, Faye and Jo. With Ariana Harner and Clark Secrest. Aurora, Colo.,
    January 18, 1999.

Untiedt, Margery, Jon, Judi, Teresa, and Linda. With Ariana Harner and
    Clark Secrest. Louisville, Colo., July 28, 1998.

Widger, Blanche Stonebraker. With Ariana Harner. Pueblo, Colo., July 11,
    1998.

———. With Clark Secrest. Pueblo, Colo., October 1993.

Yaron, Dr. Michael. Telephone interview with Ariana Harner. Denver,
    Colo., March 13, 1999.

Youkey, Eunice Frost. With Ariana Harner. McCook, Neb., July 18, 1998.

Newspapers

Major newspapers consulted are available on microfilm at the Colorado
    Historical Society or at the Denver Public Library. The *Holly (Colo.)
    Chieftain* clipping is from the personal collection of Rosemary Brown
    Cannon. Clippings from the Greeley County newspapers can be
    found at the Greeley County Historical Society in Tribune, Kan.

Denver Post: March 28 through May 6, 1931; May 23, 1931; May 31, 1931;
    June 7, 1931; June 27, 1931; July 20, 1931; July 23, 1931; November
    3, 1931; October 28, 1934; August 18, 1936; November 20, 1936;
    April 7, 1937; February 15, 1938; March 20, 1938; November 20,
    1939; February 8, 1943; January 28, 1949; March 27, 1957; March
    26, 1961; March 23, 1962; March 22, 1981.

Denver Rocky Mountain News: March 28 through April 15, 1931.

Holly (Colo.) Chieftain, April 2, 1931.

Lamar (Colo.) Daily News: March 28 through May 31, 1931; October 7, 1931; October 15, 1931; March 26, 1932.

Los Angeles Examiner: June 27, 1931; August 11, 1931.

New York Herald Tribune: May 3, 1931.

New York Times, March 28, 1931; April 2, 1931; April 8, 1931; April 16, 1931; April 30, 1931.

Tribune (Kan.) Greeley County News: April 8, 1932.

Tribune (Kan.) Greeley County Republican: April 2, 1931; March 31, 1932; November 13, 1991.

Tribune (Kan.) Greeley County Republican and the Greeley County News: September 21, 1933.

Washington Herald: May 5, 1931.

Washington Times: May 2, 1931.

Index

(Note: italic page numbers indicate photographs.)

About the Authors

Ariana Harner formerly wrote and edited for the Colorado Historical Society (now History Colorado). She received a bachelor of arts from Mount Holyoke College and a master of arts from the University of Denver. Currently, she lives and works in Denver.

Clark Secrest is a retired editor and writer, now residing in Southern California. He graduated from the universities of Denver and Missouri and wrote for *The Denver Post* and the Colorado Historical Society (now History Colorado). He is the author of *Hell's Belles*, a crime history of Denver and Colorado.